Temptations

Junior Service League of Rome, Georgia

Temptations Publications
Junior Service League of Rome, Inc.
P. O. Box 5542
Rome, Georgia 30161
404-291-8380

First Printing, October, 1985 .... 5,000 Copies

Library of Congress Catalog Card Number 85-81084
ISBN 0-9615581-0-5

Printed in the United States of America
Southern States Printing Company
Post Office Box 233
Griffin, Georgia 30224

Cookbook Committee
1982-1985

Chairman
Katie Montgomery Dempsey

Recipe Chairman
Barbara Obenshain Segars

Design Chairman
Linda Ransom James

Testing Chairman
Debbie Hulten Voss

Editing Chairman
Kathy Vogler Steinbruegge

Format Chairman
Susan Gates Farrar

Finance Chairman
Janet Farrar Griffin

Terri Huffman Booker
Claudia I. Bradley
Lee Kimbrell Hight
Christa Cline Jackson

Lynn Newton Pardue
Mary Louise Diden Payne
Ellen Rogers Smith
Nancy Loveday Smith

Fielding Hight Stutts

Supporters: Caroline Boone Alford, Fran Burt Bagley, Brenda Sermersheim Betz, Charla Bargainnier Brewster, Kendall Cobb Brock, Kathy Leary Byington, Janice Lee Carter, Jane Gray Cunningham Collier, Dianne Magruder Cumming, Nancy Burton Davis, Janice Pursley Dismuke, Theresa Hand DuPré, Sherry Tyler Finnell, Suzy Barritt Gilbert, Jan Amspoker Hackett, Sue Ellenburg Hight, Casey Nikoloric Hine, Sylvia Street Hine, LouElla McCarthney Hobgood, Barbara Hitchcock Holden, Jo Gross Huffman, Martha Edge Huffman, Debbie Henson Law, Irby Lassiter Ledbetter, Nancy Lawton Liverett, Peg Holes MacLeod, Alden Morris Maier, Marshall H. Mann, Nancy Stripling Mann, Sue Weems Mann, Nancy Dague McCallie, Aimee Daniel McNeil, Nancy Sohosky Meadows, Gayle Robinson Monk, Jackie Buffington Mooney, Pam Bagley Morgan, Marny Fulton Rhodes, Harriett Brown Rogers, Ansley Briley Saville, Jo Hickman Selman, Suzanne Jones Shapard, Elaine Hackett Smith, Nancy Sanders Starr, Sue Moser Summerall, Barbara Barbogello Triplitt, Inge Almanstoetter Weed, Betsy Eldridge Wyatt

"The object of this League shall be to foster interest among its members in the social, economic, educational, cultural and civic conditions of the community and to make efficient their volunteer service."

For fifty years since its inception in 1934, The Junior Service League of Rome, Inc., has evolved and broadened its horizons to meet the ever changing needs of the community.

During these years, the Junior Service League has continually trained its members for community service and has raised monies to finance the following projects:

... Tuberculosis Program
... School Lunchroom Program in six city schools
... Biennial "Follies" productions
... Speech School Program
... Vision Screening in area schools
... Nurses Scholarships
... Art and Music Enrichment Program in city and county schools
... Fine Arts Lecture Series
... Scholarships for Special Education
... Chieftains Museum, a National Historic Landmark
... Audiometer testing and Scoliosis screening in city and county schools
... Children's Creative Theatre
... Chieftains Road Race
... Drug Prevention Program, G.A.T.E.

Funds raised from the Sale of **Temptations** will be used in the community to finance ongoing projects and new programs in needed areas.

Fielding H. Stutts
President

TABLE OF CONTENTS

Hors d'Œuvres

Hors d'Oeuvres

Blue Cheese Mousse
Bourekakia
Brie in Pastry
Cheese Caraway Nips
Pickled Shrimp
Crab Meat Au Gratin
Sherried Crab
Island Dip
Liver Pâté
Lobster Mousse
Mushroom Pastries
Nutty Chicken Spread
Salmon Mousse with Cucumber Sauce
Shrimp Beurre
Stuffed Edam Cheese
Mushroom Caps Royale
24 Hour Cream Cheese Spread
Won Ton Willie's Egg Rolls
Chinese Sweet and Sour Sauce
HHHHOT Chinese Mustard
Cheese Straws

Blue Cheese Mousse

Truly a first class hors d'oeuvre!

Preparation: Average (Chill Overnight)
Cooking Time: 10 Minutes

6 egg yolks
6 tablespoons heavy cream
1½ tablespoons plain gelatin
¼ cup chilled white wine
¾ pound blue cheese
1½ cups heavy cream, whipped
3 egg whites, stiffly beaten
Crackers

Beat yolks and 6 tablespoons of cream together and cook over low heat until slightly thickened.

Soften gelatin in wine, then heat until dissolved. Add gelatin mixture to egg yolk mixture.

Force cheese through a sieve or grate in food processor. Add egg yolk mixture. Fold in beaten egg whites and whipped cream.

Pour into oiled 1½ quart mold and chill overnight.

Serve with crackers.

Mrs. William M. Huffman
(Jo Gross)

Bourekakia

This is a Greek word meaning cheese puffs.

Preparation: Average   **Yield:** 40 to 50 Puffs
Cooking Time: 20 Minutes

¼ pound coarsely mashed Feta cheese
1 (3 ounce) package of cream cheese
1 egg
Dash nutmeg
1 package Phyllo sheets
Melted butter

Preheat oven to 350°.

Combine cheeses, egg and nutmeg. Beat until smooth.

Work with only one sheet at a time.

Brush Phyllo sheet with melted butter and cut lengthwise into strips about four inches wide and six inches long. Stack remaining leaves and place between barely dampened kitchen towels to prevent drying.

Place scant teaspoon of filling on bottom corner of the strip. Fold corner diagonally over filling to form a triangle. Continue folding in triangles the length of the strip. (Similar to folding a flag.) Seal seam with butter. Place on ungreased cookie sheet and chill.

Bake for 20 minutes until nicely browned.

Serve warm.

Note: Phyllo sheets and filling can be frozen.

Mrs. Gordon Lee Hight, II
(Sue Ellenburg)

Brie in Pastry

A very easy, but most impressive appetizer.

Preparation: Average
Cooking Time: 15 Minutes

Serves: 12 to 14

> 1 (3 ounce) package cream cheese
> ½ stick butter or margarine
> ¾ cup all-purpose flour
> 1 (4½ ounce) package Brie cheese
> 2 egg whites (optional)

Combine cream cheese, butter and flour until it resembles small peas. Shape into a ball. Wrap in plastic wrap and chill for at least an hour or overnight. Divide dough into 2 equal pieces.

Preheat oven to 400°.

On a lightly floured surface, roll out each piece until approximately ⅛ inch thick. Cut from each piece of pastry a 6 inch circle. Place one circle on an ungreased baking sheet. Place whole cheese in center of dough. Top with remaining pastry. Pinch edges of dough together to seal.

Roll out dough scraps and cut with small cookie cutter or knife to make design. (Be creative!) Top pastry with design. Brush top of pastry with egg whites, if desired.

Bake for 15 to 17 minutes or until golden brown. Let stand for several minutes before serving.

Serve warm.

Mrs. Jim Hobgood
(LouElla McCarthney)

Cheese Caraway Nips

These keep well in a tin for drop in company.

Preparation: Average
Cooking Time: 7 to 9 Minutes

Yield: 4 Dozen

> 1 cup sifted all-purpose flour
> 2 teaspoons dry mustard (or more
>   to taste)
> 1 teaspoon salt
> ¾ cup sharp Cheddar cheese, grated
> 2 teaspoons caraway seeds
> ⅓ cup shortening
> 4 tablespoons water

Preheat oven to 450°.

Combine flour, mustard, salt, cheese and caraway seeds. Mix in shortening. Sprinkle with water. Form into two balls. Sprinkle with additional flour and refrigerate until firm.

Roll out as thinly as possible. Work quickly to keep dough cold. Cut into strips and place on ungreased cookie sheet.

Bake for 7 to 9 minutes.

Mrs. Jack Cumming
(Dianne Magruder)

Pickled Shrimp

Serve this as a finger food or as an appetizer for a seated dinner.

Preparation: Easy (Chill Overnight) **Yield:** 7 to 8 Pints
Cooking Time: 5 to 7 Minutes

> 2½ pounds peeled and deveined shrimp
> ¼ cup mixed pickling spices
> 3½ teaspoons salt
> 7 or 8 (1 pint) Mason jars
> 1 medium onion, sliced
> 7 bay leaves
> 7 to 9 tablespoons capers and juice
> 1¼ cups salad oil
> ¾ cup white vinegar
> 1½ teaspoons salt
> 2½ teaspoons celery seed
> Dash of Tabasco sauce

Cook shrimp, pickling spices and salt in boiling water until done. Drain and cool.

Alternate layers of shrimp and onion in Mason jars. Add one bay leaf and one tablespoon capers to each jar while layering.

Combine oil, vinegar, salt, celery seed and Tabasco. Mix well, then divide evenly into jars. Cover and refrigerate 24 hours.

Turn upside down once.

Ms. Kathleen Hight

Crab Meat Au Gratin

A great hors d'oeuvre with toast points or a
wonderful special occasion entrée.

Preparation: Easy
Cooking Time: 20 Minutes

Serves: 30

> 1 small bell pepper, finely chopped
> ¼ cup finely chopped onion
> 2 tablespoons butter
> 2 tablespoons flour
> 2 cups half-and-half
> 1 pound fresh crab meat, drained
> Pinch of nutmeg
> Salt and pepper to taste
> 2 cups grated sharp cheese
> Toast points

Preheat oven to 400°.

Sauté green pepper and onion in butter until translucent. Stir in flour and cook for about two minutes. Mix in half-and-half, adding crab meat and seasonings. Cook slowly until mixture thickens. Stir in one cup of cheese.

Pour into buttered 2 quart casserole dish and cover with remaining cup of cheese. Bake for 15 to 20 minutes until very hot and cheese is melted. Serve with toast points.

Individual ramekins or baking shells may be used if preparing as an entrée.

Mrs. Burgett Mooney, III
(Jackie Buffington)

Sherried Crab

Always a favorite!

Preparation: Easy   **Serves:** 30
Cooking Time: 10 Minutes

> 1 pound crab meat, preferably fresh
> 4 (3 ounce) packages cream cheese,
>   softened
> ½ cup mayonnaise
> 2 teaspoons mustard
> 1 tablespoon powdered sugar
> 1 clove garlic, pressed
> 1 tablespoon onion juice
> ½ cup cream sherry
> Sliced almonds
> Toast points

Combine all ingredients, except almonds, in a saucepan. Cook on medium heat until well-blended.

Serve in chafing dish to keep warm. Garnish with almonds. Serve with toast points.

Mrs. Leeon Rhodes
(Marny Fulton)

Island Dip

Preparation: Easy   **Yield:** One Quart
Cooking Time: None

2 egg yolks
1 teaspoon salt
1 teaspoon sugar
1 teaspoon dry mustard
¼ teaspoon paprika
1 tablespoon vinegar
3 tablespoons lemon juice
2 cups cold salad oil
1 tablespoon hot water
½ cup chili sauce
¼ cup chopped green olives
2 boiled eggs, chopped
¼ cup chopped sweet pickles

This recipe is made entirely with an electric mixer.

On high speed beat egg yolks until thick. Beat in salt, sugar, mustard, paprika, vinegar and lemon juice.

On medium speed gradually add salad oil and hot water.

On low speed add chili sauce, chopped olives, eggs and pickles.

Better if made several hours in advance and allowed to thicken.

Serve with crudités.

Mrs. Robert Rogers
(Harriett Brown)

Liver Pâté

Not a liver lover? This will change your mind!

Preparation: Easy   **Serves:** 20
Cooking Time: 20 Minutes

> ½ cup butter
> 1 medium onion, finely chopped
> 1 clove garlic, finely chopped
> 8 ounces chicken livers
> 1 bay leaf
> 1 sprig parsley
> ¼ teaspoon thyme
> 1 tablespoon brandy
> Salt and pepper to taste
> Toast points

Sauté onion and garlic in ⅛ cup of butter.

Remove from skillet and add chicken livers, bay leaf, parsley and thyme.

Cook until livers are done.

Combine livers, onions and garlic in blender or food processor. Add remaining butter slowly, then brandy. Taste for seasoning.

Pour pâté into small serving container and cover with layer of clarified butter, if desired. Refrigerate.

Serve with toast points.

Mrs. Robert W. Huff
(Egie Grant)

17

Lobster Mousse

Preparation: Average (Chill Overnight)   **Serves:** 20
Cooking Time: 5 to 7 Minutes

> 1 (10¾ ounce) can tomato soup
> 1 (¼ ounce) envelope unflavored gelatin
> 2 (3 ounce) packages cream cheese,
>   softened
> ¼ cup finely chopped celery
> ⅛ teaspoon onion salt
> Pepper to taste
> Worcestershire sauce to taste
> 1 cup mayonnaise
> 2 (6½ ounce) cans lobster or ¾ pound
>   fresh lobster meat, cooked
> Lettuce
> Parsley
> Crackers

Heat tomato soup and stir in gelatin until dissolved. Add cream cheese, beating until smooth. Add celery, onion salt, pepper and Worcestershire sauce. Fold in mayonnaise.

Break lobster into small pieces. Add to mixture.

Grease a 4 cup mold with cooking spray or rub with vegetable oil. Pour ingredients into the mold and chill for at least 8 hours or overnight.

Unmold. Serve on a bed of Boston or Bibb lettuce and garnish with parsley. Serve with crackers.

Note: Crab meat and/or shrimp may be substituted for the lobster.

Mrs. William R. Bowdoin, Jr.
(Patty Farrell)

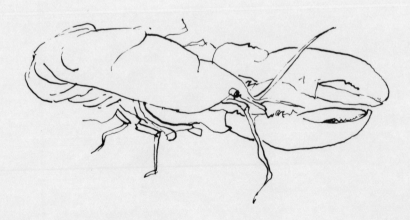

18

Mushroom Pastries

Melts in your mouth!

Preparation: Average
Cooking Time: 25 Minutes

Pastry:
½ cup butter
3 (3 ounce) packages cream cheese
1½ cups all-purpose flour

Filling:
1 large onion, finely chopped
3 tablespoons butter
½ pound mushrooms, finely chopped
½ teaspoon thyme
½ teaspoon garlic salt
Fresh ground pepper
2 tablespoons flour
¼ cup sour cream

Pastry:
Mix butter and cream cheese together. Add flour and work together until smooth. Refrigerate at least two hours.

Preheat oven to 425°.

Filling:
Sauté onion in butter. Add mushrooms and cook 3 minutes. Add spices and stir until well-blended. Sprinkle flour over mixture and stir again. Add sour cream and cook until thick.

Roll pastry thin. Cut into 3 inch circles. Spoon one teaspoon mixture onto each circle. Fold over and crimp edges.

Bake on ungreased cookie sheet for 15 minutes.

Mrs. S. David Smith, Jr.
(Nancy Loveday)

Nutty Chicken Spread

Excellent for cocktails, sandwiches or on a bed of lettuce.

Preparation: Average

Cooking Time: 1 Hour

Yield: 4 Cups

3 pounds chicken breasts
1 (8 ounce) package cream cheese,
  softened
2 tablespoons mayonnaise
¾ cup chopped pecans or walnuts
1 tablespoon grated onion
2 tablespoons sweet pickle juice
1 cup finely chopped celery
⅛ teaspoon curry powder
Salt and pepper to taste
Green and ripe olives
Parsley
Cherry tomatoes
Twist of lemon
Crackers

Cook chicken in salted water to cover until tender. Remove from broth, reserving broth. Cool. Bone chicken and grind or chop fine.

Combine cream cheese and mayonnaise, beating well. Add pecans, onion, pickle juice, celery, curry powder, salt and pepper. Stir until well-blended.

Combine chicken and cream cheese mixture. Blend well. Add ¼ to ½ cup chicken broth to desired consistency. Mixture will thicken when chilled.

Spoon spread into a mold which has been rubbed with mayonnaise. Chill. Unmold and garnish with olives, parsley, cherry tomatoes and twist of lemon. Serve with crackers.

Note: Chicken will be more moist if cooked and boned the day before using and placed in the broth to chill.

Mrs. James McCallie
(Nancy Dague)

Salmon Mousse with Cucumber Sauce

Rich and delicious!

Preparation: Average
Cooking Time: None

Serves: 20

Mousse:
- 2 cups flaked salmon
- 3 tablespoons lemon juice
- 3 tablespoons mayonnaise
- ¾ teaspoon salt
- ⅛ teaspoon cayenne pepper
- 1 envelope unflavored gelatin
- ½ cup cold water
- ½ cup heavy cream, whipped
- Crackers

Sauce:
- 1 cup sour cream
- ½ cup finely chopped cucumber
- 2 teaspoons minced chives
- ¾ teaspoon dill
- 2 tablespoons minced parsley
- 1 tablespoon grated onion
- 1 teaspoon lemon juice

Mousse:
Combine salmon, lemon juice, mayonnaise, salt and cayenne pepper. Soften gelatin in cold water, then dissolve over low heat. Cool and combine with salmon mixture. Fold in cream.

Chill in one mold or individual molds which have been rinsed well in cold water and coated with a thin layer of mayonnaise. (May chill in serving bowl if not using mold.)

Cucumber Sauce:
Combine all ingredients and chill. Unmold mousse, pour sauce over it and serve with crackers.

Note: Serves 8 as a first course.

Mrs. Edward W. Hine, Jr.
(Casey Nikoloric)

Shrimp Beurre

Shrimply delicious!

Preparation: Easy (Chill Overnight) **Serves:** 30
Cooking Time: 5 Minutes

**4 pounds shrimp, cooked, peeled
  and deveined
1 medium white onion, finely chopped
1 cup butter, melted
⅓ cup lemon juice
Salt and pepper to taste
Dry mustard to taste
2 ounces brandy
Fresh parsley
Melba toast**

Mince shrimp or chop in a food processor until crumbly. Add remaining ingredients and mix until a paste is formed. Pack mixture into a greased mold. Chill overnight.

Unmold, garnish with parsley and serve with Melba toast.

Mrs. M. Dwayne Collier
(Jane Gray Cunningham)

Stuffed Edam Cheese

A once popular appetizer that needs to be enjoyed again!

Preparation: Easy
Cooking Time: None

1 (7 to 8 ounce) round Edam cheese
¼ cup butter
½ teaspoon dry mustard
¼ cup chopped green olives
2 teaspoons minced onion
2 teaspoons dry white wine
2 teaspoons caraway seeds
Dash of Tabasco sauce
Crackers

Scoop out inside of cheese leaving shell ¼ inch thick. In a food processor combine cheese with remaining ingredients. Mix well and spoon mixture into cheese shell.

Serve with light buttery crackers.

Mrs. Roy Mann
(Sue Weems)

Mushroom Caps Royale

A different flair for your stuffed mushrooms! Serve also as a meat accompaniment.

Preparation: Average　　　　　　　　　　　　　　　　　　**Serves:** 6
Cooking Time: 15 Minutes

> **12 to 14 extra large fresh whole**
> **mushrooms**
> **¼ cup chopped green onions**
> **¼ cup butter or margarine**
> **¼ cup crumbled blue cheese**
> **⅓ cup dry fine bread crumbs**
> **Salt and pepper to taste**

Preheat oven to 350°.

Remove stems from mushrooms. Chop stems and cook with onions in butter until tender, not brown. Add cheese, 2 tablespoons of the bread crumbs and salt and pepper to taste.

Fill mushroom caps with mixture. Sprinkle with the remaining crumbs. Place on baking sheet.

Bake for 12 minutes.

Mrs. William M. Huffman
(Jo Gross)

24 Hour Cream Cheese Spread

*Be sure to make a day ahead to get the full benefit
of the flavor.*

Preparation: Easy (Chill Overnight)   **Serves:** 20
Cooking Time: None

> 2 (8 ounce) packages cream cheese,
>   softened
> 1/3 cup mayonnaise
> 3 spring onions, finely chopped
>   (including tops)
> Pinch of salt
> 1 cup chopped pecans
> Fresh parsley
> Paprika
> Whole wheat crackers

In food processor, blend cream cheese and mayonnaise. Add chopped onions and salt. Blend until smooth, about 2 minutes.

Place in a serving dish. Chop parsley and mix with chopped pecans. Place on top of cream cheese mixture and sprinkle with paprika. Chill overnight.

Serve with crackers.

Mrs. William R. Bowdoin, Jr.
(Patty Farrell)

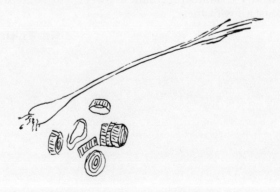

Won Ton Willie's Egg Rolls

These are some of the best egg rolls that you'll ever put in your mouth!

Preparation: Somewhat Difficult   **Yield:** 12 Large Egg Rolls
Cooking Time: Approximately 10 Minutes

3 cups bean sprouts
2 cups shredded bok choy
1 medium onion, shredded
1 cup shredded water chestnuts, drained
1 cup bamboo shoots, drained
½ cup shredded mushrooms
3 teaspoons oil
1 pound pork, minced
1 teaspoon ginger powder
½ teaspoon sugar
½ teaspoon salt
½ teaspoon monosodium glutamate
3 tablespoons soy sauce
1 package egg roll wrappers
½ cup water
1 tablespoon cornstarch
2 to 3 cups oil for frying

Prepare all vegetables. Heat 3 teaspoons oil, sauté meat and spices. Set aside. Briefly stir fry vegetables. They must be crisp.

Spread 1½ heaping tablespoons of filling mixture on each egg roll wrapper. Fold sides in and roll. Moisten edges with mixture of cornstarch and water.

Heat oil for deep frying and fry until rolls are light brown. Drain.

Note: Other types of meat may be used in place of the pork such as chicken, beef, ham, shrimp or crab meat.

Hint: Use following Chinese Sweet and Sour Sauce and HHHHot Chinese Mustard with these.

Mr. William T. Segars

Chinese Sweet and Sour Sauce

Preparation: Easy
Cooking Time: 10 Minutes

Yield: Approximately 5 Cups

3 cups apricot nectar
1 cup plus 2 tablespoons sugar
1 cup vinegar
¾ cup crushed pineapple with juice
1 teaspoon salt
⅛ cup maraschino cherry juice
1 tablespoon grenadine
3 tablespoons gelatin
½ cup water

Simmer apricot nectar, sugar, vinegar, pineapple with juice, salt, maraschino cherry juice and grenadine for about 5 minutes.

Add gelatin and ½ cup water and simmer for 5 more minutes.

Mr. William T. Segars

HHHHot Chinese Mustard

Preparation: Easy
Cooking Time: 10 Minutes (Let Stand Overnight)

Yield: ¾ Cup

¼ cup dry mustard
¼ cup boiling water
1 teaspoon sugar
1 tablespoon oil
2 teaspoons wine
1 teaspoon soy sauce

Mix all ingredients together.

Cover and let stand for one day before serving.

Mr. William T. Segars

Cheese Straws

Good with soup, salad or cocktails.

Preparation: Average   **Yield:** 3 Dozen
Cooking Time: 10 to 12 Minutes

> 1 pound New York sharp Cheddar
>   cheese, grated
> ¼ cup butter
> ¼ cup margarine
> 1 teaspoon salt
> ½ teaspoon red pepper
> 3 cups unsifted all-purpose flour

Preheat oven to 350°.

In food processor, combine butter, margarine and cheese. Process until creamed. Add salt, red pepper and flour. Process until dough forms a ball.

Press out with cookie press using flat disk with serations on top. Cut into desired lengths.

Bake on ungreased cookie sheet for 10 to 12 minutes. Cool and serve.

Note: Dough may be frozen.

Mrs. Roy Alford
(Caroline Boone)

Soups and Salads

Soups and Salads

Spicy Cream of Mushroom Soup
Favorite Oyster Stew
Georgia Brunswick Stew
Cheesy Chowder
Chilled Cherry Soup
Crab Meat Bisque
Norwegian Cauliflower Soup
Shrimp Gumbo
Artichoke and Rice Salad
Italian Pasta Salad
Ladies Club Tuna Salad
Orange Romaine Salad
Salad with Brie Dressing
Special Chicken Salad
Vegetable Aspic with Horseradish Sauce
Classic Roquefort Dressing
Company Bacon Dressing
Creamy Spinach Salad Dressing

Spicy Cream of Mushroom Soup

Get your taste buds primed with this first course.

Preparation: Average   **Serves:** 2 to 4
Cooking Time: 45 Minutes

½ cup butter
1 pound mushrooms, chopped
½ small onion, minced
¾ cup flour
½ cup white wine
1 quart chicken broth
1 pint half-and-half
½ teaspoon nutmeg
¼ teaspoon cayenne pepper
½ teaspoon paprika
Salt and pepper to taste

Heat butter in a heavy skillet. Add mushrooms and onions. Sauté until lightly colored.

Add flour. Mix and cook covered 2 minutes without browning. Add wine and chicken broth. Mix to dissolve lumps of flour. Add cream.

Allow to simmer 30 minutes. Season with spices.

Note: Soup may be prepared ahead and reheated in a double boiler.

Mrs. Steve Stutts
(Fielding Hight)

Favorite Oyster Stew

Must be made when fresh oysters are available.

Preparation: Easy
Cooking Time: 15 Minutes

2 cups milk
½ cup butter
½ teaspoon salt
½ teaspoon black pepper
¼ teaspoon paprika
½ pint raw oysters, reserve liquor
Oyster crackers

Heat milk with butter, salt, pepper and paprika until hot, but not boiling.

Add oysters and liquor to the hot milk mixture and stir until the edges of the oysters begin to curl.

Remove from heat and serve immediately with oyster crackers.

Mrs. Boyce S. Brice
(Maxine Strom)

Georgia Brunswick Stew

A real crowd pleaser!

Preparation: Average
Cooking Time: 3 Hours

Serves: 12 to 16

2 whole chicken breasts
6 to 8 chicken thighs
1½ pounds stew beef
4 lean pork chops, trimmed
1½ cups smoke-flavored
    barbecue sauce
1½ cups water
4 medium baking potatoes,
    peeled and diced
3 large onions, chopped
1 (17 ounce) can Lima
    beans, drained

2 (14½ ounce) cans stewed
    tomatoes, mashed or
    blended
6 ounces frozen or fresh
    cut okra
2 (17 ounce) cans cream style
    corn
½ cup Worcestershire sauce
1½ cups ketchup
½ teaspoon cayenne pepper
    or hot sauce
Salt and pepper to taste

Put all meat and barbecue sauce in pressure cooker with 1½ cups of water. Process for 45 minutes.

Shred meat and discard all bones and chicken skin. Set meat aside.

Strain stock into a covered 8 quart soup pot. Add potatoes and onions. Cover and cook on medium heat for 15 minutes.

Add all remaining ingredients and meats. Bring to a bubbly boil while stirring. Cover and simmer at least 2 hours or until potatoes are done. Stir often to avoid scorching.

Note: Better the second day. You can remove the fat that has collected on top.

Mrs. Charles Hight, Jr.
(Lee Kimbrell)

Cheesy Chowder

A cheese lover's delight!

Preparation: Easy
Cooking Time: 30 Minutes

1 medium onion, chopped
2 stalks celery, chopped
2 tablespoons butter, melted
6 medium potatoes, cubed
2 carrots, sliced
3 cups water
5 chicken-flavored bouillon
    cubes
¾ teaspoon seasoned salt

½ teaspoon whole thyme
½ teaspoon rosemary, crushed
Dash garlic powder
2 cups milk
2 to 4 cups Longhorn Cheddar
    cheese, shredded

Sauté onion and celery in butter in large pot until tender.

Add the next 8 ingredients, cover and simmer about 20 minutes or until vegetables are tender.

Remove from heat. Using potato masher, mash vegetables. Blend in milk and cheese. (Add amount of cheese to taste.) Heat, stirring constantly, until cheese is melted.

Mrs. Gary R. Schlenk
(Lisa Baumgartner)

Chilled Cherry Soup

An elegant first course for a formal dinner party.

Preparation: Average   **Serves:** 6
Cooking Time: 10 Minutes

3 cups cold water
1 cup sugar
1 cinnamon stick
4 cups (2 cans) pie cherries,
    drained
1 tablespoon arrowroot
2 tablespoons cold water
¼ cup heavy cream, chilled
¾ cup red wine, chilled
Whipped cream (optional)

In a 2 quart pot combine water, sugar and cinnamon stick. Bring to a boil. Add drained cherries to boiling water.

In a small cup or bowl, mix arrowroot with 2 tablespoons cold water. Mix to a paste. Beat arrowroot into the cherries and water, stirring constantly. Bring soup to just below boiling.

Immediately reduce heat to low and simmer about 2 minutes, stirring all the while until soup is clear and slightly thickened. Pour into a glass, ceramic or plastic container. Cool and then chill in refrigerator.

Just before serving, stir in cream and wine. Garnish with a dollop of whipped cream, if desired.

Dr. Marshall H. Mann

Crab Meat Bisque

*This delicious bisque can be made ahead of time
and frozen, adding seafood just before serving.*

Preparation: Average　　　　　　　　　　　　　　　　**Serves:** 6 to 8
Cooking Time: 1 Hour and 20 Minutes

2 pounds crab meat
¼ pound butter
2 cups finely chopped onion
3 cloves crushed garlic
1 cup chopped celery
1 cup chopped green pepper
¼ cup bacon grease
½ cup flour
2 (16 ounce) cans tomatoes
2 tablespoons lemon juice
3 bay leaves
⅛ teaspoon thyme
6 tablespoons tomato sauce
½ cup finely chopped parsley
Salt and pepper to taste
Cayenne pepper and Tabasco sauce
　　　　to taste

Check crab meat for shells and set aside.

Melt butter in a pan and brown onions, garlic, celery and green pepper. Set aside. In a heavy pot make a dark brown roux using bacon grease and flour. Add tomatoes, lemon juice, bay leaves, thyme and tomato sauce. Stir well and add cooked onions, celery and green pepper. Stir well, cover and simmer about one hour or until mixture starts to thicken.

Add remaining seasonings to taste. Stir in crab meat and cook over low heat for 10 more minutes, stirring occasionally. Remove bay leaves and serve immediately.

Note: Shrimp may be substituted for crab meat.

Mrs. Craig Voss
(Debbie Hulten)

Norwegian Cauliflower Soup

Cauliflower never had it so good!

Preparation: Easy
Cooking Time: 30 Minutes

Serves: 6 to 8

> 1 large head of cauliflower
> 1 tablespoon butter
> 1½ tablespoons flour
> 4 cups boiling water
> 4 chicken bouillon cubes
> ½ teaspoon salt
> ¼ teaspoon white pepper
> 1 egg yolk, beaten
> ¼ cup heavy cream

Clean cauliflower and break into flowerets. Place in a pot, cover with water and bring to a boil. Cook 10 minutes.

Drain and purée in processor or blender.

Melt butter in pan. Stir in flour. Dissolve bouillon cubes in 4 cups of boiling water. Gradually stir into butter and flour mixture. Cook, stirring well, until slightly thickened. Stir in puréed cauliflower, salt and pepper.

In a small bowl mix egg yolk, cream and add 3 tablespoons of hot soup. Blend well and stir into soup. Serve hot.

Mrs. M. Dwayne Collier
(Jane Gray Cunningham)

Shrimp Gumbo

The trick is the roux — be careful not to let it burn.

Preparation: Average **Serves:** 8 to 10
Cooking Time: 1 Hour and 40 Minutes

1½ to 2 pounds fresh shrimp
½ teaspoon crab boil
5 tablespoons bacon drippings
5 tablespoons flour
1 large onion, chopped
2 pounds fresh okra, chopped
   or 1 box frozen okra,
   thawed
3 stalks celery, chopped
2 tablespoons chopped
   parsley
1 (16 ounce) can whole
   tomatoes
1 cup uncooked rice

1 large bell pepper,
   chopped
1 clove garlic, mashed
1 teaspoon salt
½ teaspoon pepper
¼ teaspoon dried thyme
¼ teaspoon ground oregano
2 whole bay leaves

Cover shrimp with water and crab boil. Cook until tender (about 10 minutes). Drain and **SAVE WATER.** Peel shrimp and set aside.

In an iron pot or Dutch oven, make a roux with bacon drippings and flour. Add the chopped onion and sauté. Add okra and cook about 10 minutes over medium heat, stirring constantly.

Add shrimp water, celery, parsley, tomatoes, bell pepper, garlic, salt and pepper. Simmer 1 hour.

Add thyme, oregano, bay leaves and peeled shrimp. Cook for another 20 minutes.

Prepare rice according to package directions. Remove bay leaves and serve gumbo in a bowl over rice.

Note: Proper preparation of roux is important. Use an iron skillet, combine flour and drippings and brown very slowly over low heat stirring constantly until dark chocolate brown. If there is even a hint of scorched or burned roux, discard and begin again.

Mrs. D. Leon Sproles
(Susan Scott)

Artichoke and Rice Salad

A salad for all seasons.

Preparation: Easy (Chill Overnight)   **Serves:** 8
Cooking Time: 20 Minutes

> 1 package chicken-flavored rice
> 2 jars marinated artichokes
> 4 spring onions
> ½ bell pepper
> 12 green olives
> ⅓ cup mayonnaise
> ⅓ teaspoon curry powder

Put rice and 2¾ cups of water in saucepan. Bring to a boil. Reduce heat, cover and cook 20 minutes or until all the water is absorbed. Cool.

Drain artichokes and save juice.

Chop bell pepper, onions and olives. Cut artichokes in half. Mix together and add to rice. Blend well.

Stir together mayonnaise, curry powder and artichoke juice. Mix this with other ingredients.

Chill overnight and serve cold. May garnish with black olives.

Mrs. Peter Holden
(Sandy Powell)

Italian Pasta Salad

Lovely in hot weather.

Preparation: Easy
Cooking Time: None

Serves: 10

3 to 4 cups cooked large tube
  type pasta, pasta wheels or
  corkscrew pasta
½ cup thinly sliced black olives
1 small purple onion, thinly sliced
1 pint basket cherry tomatoes,
  halved
3 ounces pepperoni, thinly sliced
  and bite-sized
¼ pound Mozzarella cheese, cubed
2 stalks celery, thinly sliced
½ bell pepper, thinly sliced
1 carrot, thinly sliced
1 pint basket mushrooms, thinly
  sliced
1 small jar pimientos, drained
1 can artichoke hearts, drained
  and quartered
Fresh ground pepper to taste
Basil to taste
Italian dressing (of your choice)
Parmesan cheese, grated

Cook pasta al dente.

Combine all but last 2 ingredients. Pour on your favorite Italian dressing and top with Parmesan cheese. Chill until ready to serve.

Mrs. Cyrus Overman
(Shirley Ferguson)

Ladies Club Tuna Salad

Better if made the day before.

Preparation: Easy (Chill Overnight)   **Serves:** 8
Cooking Time: 30 Minutes

    1 box white and wild rice
    2 (6½ ounce) cans water-packed
        white tuna, drained
    ½ cup chopped celery
    ½ cup chopped green pepper
    4 green onions, chopped
    1 cup mayonnaise
    ½ cup sour cream
    Salt, pepper, cayenne pepper
        to taste
    Lettuce
    Chopped cashews

Cook rice according to package directions. Allow to cool. Combine rice and remaining ingredients, except cashews. Refrigerate overnight.

Serve in lettuce cups. Garnish with cashews.

Mrs. Walter Matthews
(Cheryl Perry)

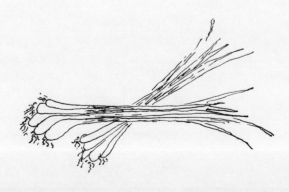

Orange Romaine Salad

Delightfully different.

Preparation: Easy

Serves: 6 to 8

Cooking Time: None

Salad:
- 1 large head romaine lettuce, torn
- 4 small onions, thinly sliced
- 1 (11 ounce) can mandarin oranges
- 8 slices bacon, fried crisp and crumbled
- ½ to 1 cup toasted almonds

Poppy Seed Dressing:
- ½ cup sugar
- ⅔ cup vegetable oil
- 1 teaspoon prepared mustard
- 2 tablespoons poppy seeds
- ¼ cup vinegar
- 1 teaspoon salt

Place salad ingredients in a large salad bowl.

Combine all dressing ingredients in a jar. Cover tightly and shake vigorously. Pour over salad and toss gently.

Mrs. Tom Lumpkin
(Diane Freeman)

Salad with Brie Dressing

A nice salad for entertaining. Easy but elegant.

Preparation: Easy
Cooking Time: 30 Minutes

Serves: 10

Salad:
1 medium head curly endive
1 medium head iceberg lettuce
1 medium head romaine lettuce
Garlic croutons

Dressing:
½ cup olive oil
4 teaspoons minced green onion
1 large garlic clove, minced
½ cup sherry wine vinegar
2 tablespoons fresh lemon juice
1½ tablespoons Dijon mustard
10 ounces Brie cheese
Freshly ground pepper

Salad:
Wash and drain lettuce. Tear into bite-sized pieces.

Dressing:
Remove rind from Brie. Cut cheese into small pieces and allow it to soften to room temperature.

Heat oil in skillet over low heat for almost 10 minutes. Add onion and garlic and sauté about 5 minutes or until tender.

Blend in vinegar, lemon juice and mustard. Add cheese and stir until smooth. Season to taste with pepper.

Toss warm dressing with lettuce and croutons. Serve immediately.

Special Chicken Salad

The carrots make the difference.

Preparation: Easy
Cooking Time: None

Serves: 4 to 6

1 tablespoon fresh lemon juice
1 cup mayonnaise
2 cups diced cooked chicken
1 cup shredded carrots
¾ cup diced celery
½ cup slivered almonds
2 tablespoons minced onion
Salt and pepper to taste
Dash curry powder (optional)
Lettuce

Stir lemon juice into mayonnaise. Toss with chicken, carrots, celery, almonds and onions. Season to taste, chill and serve on a bed of lettuce.

Mrs. Wayne Knighton
(Jane Collier)

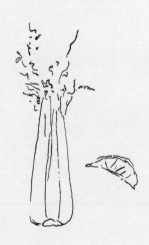

Vegetable Aspic with Horseradish Sauce

Even men will eat this aspic. The accompanying sauce is also good with beef.

Preparation: Average   **Serves:** 8 to 10
Cooking Time: 10 Minutes

Aspic:
- 1 (16 ounce) can small whole green beans (reserve juice)
- 1 (16 ounce) can artichoke hearts
- 1 (16 ounce) can early peas (reserve juice)
- 2 envelopes plain gelatin
- ¼ cup cold water
- 1 teaspoon salt
- ½ cup combination lemon juice, apple cider vinegar and tarragon vinegar
- 1 teaspoon sugar
- 1 tablespoon chopped parsley
- 1½ teaspoons summer savory, dried

Fluffy Horseradish Sauce:
- 2 egg yolks
- 2 tablespoons white wine vinegar
- 2 tablespoons prepared horseradish
- 1 tablespoon sugar
- 1 tablespoon Dijon mustard
- 1 tablespoon water
- 1 teaspoon salt
- ½ cup whipping cream

Aspic:

Drain vegetables, reserving juice from peas and beans. Quarter artichoke hearts. Sprinkle gelatin into ¼ cup cold water. Combine gelatin with 2 cups of reserved juices which have been brought to a boil. Add remaining ingredients except for drained vegetables. Stir. Allow to cool.

Pour gelatin mixture into lightly oiled mold. Add vegetables, arranging evenly. Refrigerate until congealed. Serve with Fluffy Horseradish Sauce.

Fluffy Horseradish Sauce:

Beat egg yolks lightly over top of double boiler until thick. Add everything but whipping cream and stir for approximately 5 to 7 minutes or until thick. Do not let water in boiler reach a boil. Cool. Beat whipping cream until thick and fold together. Refrigerate until ready to serve.

Mrs. William Davidson
(Sue Ann Smith)

Classic Roquefort Dressing

Preparation: Easy   **Yield:** 1 Quart
Cooking Time: None

12 ounces Roquefort or blue cheese
1 teaspoon garlic powder
12 ounces mayonnaise
4 ounces sour cream
2 tablespoons vinegar
2 tablespoons Worcestershire sauce
Tabasco sauce to taste
Salt and pepper to taste

Place all ingredients in blender or food processor on medium speed until well-blended.

Keep refrigerated.

Mrs. Robley D. Evans
(Mary Kay Lattimore)

46

Company Bacon Dressing

Preparation: Easy   **Serves:** 6
Cooking Time: 20 Minutes

> ⅓ **pound sliced bacon**
> **4 eggs**
> ⅓ **cup sugar**
> **1 teaspoon salt**
> ⅓ **cup vinegar**
> ⅓ **cup water**

Cut bacon slices into pieces and fry until crisp and then set aside.

Beat eggs. Add remaining ingredients to eggs. Stir mixture into skillet with bacon and drippings. Cook over low heat until thickened.

While warm, add to leaf lettuce, endive, spinach or any salad greens.

Mrs. Robert K. Finnell, III
(Sherry Plyler)

Creamy Spinach Salad Dressing

Unusual, but delicious.

Preparation: Easy   **Serves:** 6 to 8
Cooking Time: None

½ cup mayonnaise
2 small onions, grated or
    finely diced
4 tablespoons grated Parmesan
    cheese
4 tablespoons honey, sugar or
    maple syrup
8 tablespoons oil
4 tablespoons wine vinegar
1 teaspoon thyme
1 teaspoon garlic salt
1 teaspoon salad herbs

Mix all dressing ingredients together and shake or stir well.

This recipe keeps in the refrigerator for weeks.

Hint: Serve this dressing with fresh spinach leaves garnished with sliced raw mushrooms, raw onion rings, mandarin orange slices, bacon bits and chopped hard-cooked egg.

Mrs. Gordon Holden
(Barbara Hitchcock)

Entrées

Entrées

Cold Stuffed Tenderloin
Dove with Sausage Stuffing
Elegantly Easy Chicken
Fettucine Alla Parmesan
Charcoal Broiled Quail
Pheasant with Sage Leaves
"7 Boy" Curry
Old Fashioned Chicken Pie
Pasta Alla Melanzane
Rolled Leg of Lamb with Herbs
Simply Scampi
Shrimp Mikanos
Veal Provençal
Veal Raleigh
Sweet and Sour Pot Roast
Barbecued Ham Slices
Reuben Casserole
Marinated Pork Chops
Plum Sauce for Roast Lamb
Apricot Honey Glaze
Lemon Basting Sauce
Fourth of July Barbecue Sauce
Steak Sauce

Cold Stuffed Tenderloin

Elegant summer entrée!

Preparation: Average
Cooking Time: 45 Minutes

Serves: 8 to 12

1 stalk celery, chopped
1 carrot, chopped
1 medium onion, chopped
2 tablespoons butter
Whole beef tenderloin
2 tablespoons butter
Freshly ground pepper
½ pound bacon, cut into ¼ inch cubes
1 tablespoon olive oil
2 or more cloves garlic, pressed
1 cup sour cream
1½ tablespoons reserved pan juice
1 tablespoon grated onion
1 tablespoon chopped chives
White pepper

Preheat oven to 450°.

Combine celery, carrot, onion and 2 tablespoons butter. Sauté in bottom of roasting pan until soft. Remove fat membrane from meat and place meat on roasting pan with ends tucked under. Rub with 2 tablespoons butter and sprinkle with freshly ground pepper. Roast until desired doneness is reached with meat thermometer. **Reserve** 1½ tablespoons of strained pan juice. Cool meat completely in refrigerator.

Fry bacon in oil with garlic until crisp. Drain. Combine sour cream, reserved pan juice, onion and chives. Add bacon, salt and white pepper to taste.

About 2 hours before serving, remove a wedge the length of the tenderloin from top of tenderloin. Wedge should be 2 inches wide and 1 inch deep. Fill cavity with sour cream mixture and trim meat from wedge into ¾ inch squares. Reassemble in a checkerboard pattern on top of tenderloin.

Keep refrigerated until 20 minutes before serving. Slice 1½ inches thick.

Mrs. Lynn Dempsey
(Katie Montgomery)

Dove with Sausage Stuffing

Preparation: Easy   **Serves:** 6
Cooking Time: 1 Hour and 15 Minutes

18 doves, breast only
½ cup butter
1 tablespoon sage
1½ pounds mild sausage
18 slices bacon
18 toothpicks
Salt and pepper to taste

Preheat oven to 300°.

Salt and pepper dove breasts generously. Brown on all sides in melted butter. Remove and drain.

Mix sage with sausage. Fill each breast cavity with sausage.

Wrap each dove with bacon slice to hold in sausage and secure with a toothpick.

Place dove on a rack in a baking pan. Cover with foil. Bake 1 hour.

Mrs. William A. DuPré, Jr.
(Theresa Hand)

52

Elegantly Easy Chicken

The name says it all!

Preparation: Easy
Cooking Time: 1 Hour 30 Minutes

Serves: 6

> **Chicken pieces, skinned and washed
>   (legs, thighs, halved breasts)**
> **Seasoned salt**
> **Lemon pepper**
> **Garlic powder**
> **Powdered ginger**
> **White wine**
> **1 (8 ounce) container fresh mushrooms,
>   sliced**

Preheat oven to 325°.

Place chicken pieces, bone-side down, in shallow pan so chicken pieces do not touch. Sprinkle liberally with seasoned salt, lemon pepper and garlic powder. Sprinkle lightly with ginger.

Bake for 1 to 1½ hours. After first 20 minutes add white wine to cover bottom of pan. Baste every 20 minutes, scraping bottom of pan. Add small amount of wine if needed, but chicken should glaze brown. Sprinkle with mushrooms before last basting. Do not overcook mushrooms. Baste after removing from oven.

Mrs. Harlan Starr
(Nancy Marchant Sanders)

Fettucine Alla Parmesan

Virginia ham may be substituted for prosciutto.

Preparation: Easy   **Serves:** 2 to 4
Cooking Time: 25 Minutes

> ⅓ cup whipped butter
> 3 cloves garlic, crushed
> 2 tablespoons minced prosciutto
> ⅓ cup cooked green peas
> ½ cup heavy cream
> 1 pound Fettucine noodles, cooked
>   al dente
> 1 egg, slightly beaten
> 4 tablespoons freshly grated
>   Parmesan cheese

Melt butter in saucepan and add garlic. When butter sizzles, add prosciutto and peas, then cream. Add pasta, whole egg and cheese.

Toss gently with 2 large spoons until cheese is melted. Serve immediately.

Mrs. Richard Sargent
(Ruthann Kerce)

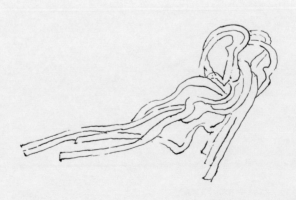

54

Charcoal Broiled Quail

Preparation: Easy
Cooking Time: 30 Minutes

Serves: 6

¼ cup butter or margarine, melted
1 cup vinegar
1 cup water
5 tablespoons honey
1 tablespoon Worcestershire sauce
1 teaspoon seasoned salt
1½ teaspoons lemon pepper
Dash of Tabasco sauce
6 quail

Mix first 8 ingredients to form marinade. Pour over quail and let stand for at least one hour. Cook quail on charcoal grill at low to medium heat for 30 minutes, basting occasionally with marinade.

Mrs. Lloyd Summer, Jr.
(Virginia Barron)

Pheasant with Sage Leaves

A hunter's delight!

Preparation: Average
Cooking Time: 2 Hours

Serves: 6 to 8

> 4 pheasant, dressed
> 1 pound thick-sliced bacon
> 1 cup fresh sage leaves
>   (2 jars dry may be
>   substituted)
> 1 clove garlic, minced
> ½ teaspoon salt
> ¼ teaspoon pepper

Preheat oven to 350°.

Dice ⅓ pound of bacon into ¼ inch pieces. Add garlic, ¼ cup sage leaves, salt and pepper. Mix well. Stuff each bird with mixture and truss.

Cover each bird with remaining sage leaves and whole slices of bacon. Wrap individually in foil.

Place birds in roasting pan and bake for 2 hours.

The aroma alone is wonderful!

Note: Grouse may be substituted.

Mr. Steve Stutts

"7 Boy" Curry

A truly different chicken dish that will be a smashing success with your dinner guests.

Preparation: Average
Cooking Time: 30 to 40 Minutes

Serves: 6 to 8

Chicken:
- 4 to 5 pounds chicken (breasts and thighs)
- 6 tablespoons oil
- 2 whole red chiles (crumbled)
- Dash ground cloves
- 5 dashes ground cardamom
- 1 onion, chopped
- 2 large garlic cloves, minced
- 5 to 6 teaspoons curry powder
- ¾ cup plain yogurt
- 1 (1 pound, 12 ounce) can Italian tomatoes
- Salt and pepper to taste
- Juice of one lemon

Pilaf:
- 1 cup raw rice
- 1 (2 ounce) jar pine nuts
- 1 cup raisins

Various Condiments (Boys):
- Plain yogurt
- Coconut
- Bean sprouts
- Chopped onions
- Chopped tomatoes
- Chopped peanuts
- Chutney

Chicken:
Brown chicken in oil.

Remove chicken from pan. Add the next five ingredients and cook 5 to 10 minutes. Mix curry powder and yogurt and add to above seasonings. Add chicken and tomatoes. Cook briskly for about 10 minutes.

Cover, lower temperature and cook until tender. Add salt and pepper. When ready to serve, add juice of one lemon.

Pilaf:
While chicken simmers, cook rice according to package directions and stir in pine nuts and raisins during the last 5 minutes of cooking.

Serve on a large platter with rice garnished with one or more of the condiments listed above.

Note: Almonds may be used instead of pine nuts.

Mrs. John S. Husser
(Esther Ransom)

Old-Fashioned Chicken Pie

Some things never go out of style.

Preparation: Average
Cooking Time: 1 Hour and 30 Minutes

Serves: 10

> 2 broiler fryers (2½ pounds each)
> Water
> 2 teaspoons salt
> ¼ teaspoon pepper
> 1 package frozen peas
> 2 cups sliced carrots
> ¼ cup margarine
> 6 tablespoons flour
> 1½ cups biscuit mix
> ½ cup sour cream
> 1 egg
> 2 teaspoons sesame seeds

Place chicken in large kettle. Add 2 cups water, salt, pepper and carrots. Heat to boiling. Reduce heat, cover and simmer for 45 minutes. Add peas, simmer for another 15 minutes or until chicken is tender. Remove chicken and cool. Skim fat from broth, reserving 2 tablespoons fat.

Melt butter with fat in a medium-sized pan. Stir in flour. Cook until bubbly, stirring constantly. Add broth, continue cooking, stirring until gravy thickens and bubbles 1 minute.

When chickens are cool, remove skin and slip meat from bones. Cut into small pieces. Stir into gravy. Pour into a 2 quart oblong baking dish.

Combine biscuit mix and sour cream in a bowl. Stir to form a stiff dough. Turn out onto a lightly floured board and roll out dough ½ inch thick. Cut into strips.

Make lattice design on top of chicken mixture and place strips on edges of dish, pinching dough to make a rim. Cut slits near center to let steam escape. Combine egg with 1 tablespoon water with a fork until well-blended. Brush over strips and sprinkle with sesame seeds.

Bake in preheated 400° oven for 30 minutes or until chicken mixture is bubbly and crust is golden.

Mrs. David Morgan
(Pam Bagley)

Pasta Alla Melanzane

A special eggplant dish! Also can be used as an accompaniment.

Preparation: Average   **Serves:** 6 to 8
Cooking Time: 30 Minutes

> 1 large or 2 small eggplant (melanzane)
> 2 tablespoons olive oil
> 2 tablespoons margarine
> 2 medium onions, chopped
> 2 bell peppers, chopped
> 1 Jalapeño pepper, finely minced
>   (optional)
> Fresh garlic, pressed or garlic
>   powder to taste
> Seasoned salt
> Lemon pepper
> 1 tablespoon vinegar
> 1 teaspoon sugar
> 2 quarts of tomatoes, drained, peeled
>   and chopped
> 1 (12 ounce) package of vermicelli or
>   thin spaghetti
> Grated Parmesan cheese

Peel and cube eggplant placing in a bowl of cold salted water and set aside.

Sauté onions and peppers in heavy pot in olive oil and margarine until soft. Add drained eggplant and tomatoes. Add all seasonings, adjusting to taste where amounts are not listed.

Cover and bring to a boil. Uncover and simmer to sauce consistency.

Cook pasta according to package directions immediately before serving. Do not rinse.

Serve sauce on hot pasta and dress with grated cheese.

Mrs. Harlan Starr
(Nancy Marchant Sanders)

Rolled Leg of Lamb with Herbs

Preparation: Average   **Serves:** 8
Cooking Time: 2 to 3 Hours

> **6 to 8 pound leg of lamb, boned**
> **½ cup fresh minced parsley**
> **2 cloves garlic, minced**
> **½ teaspoon sage**
> **1 teaspoon rosemary**
> **2 teaspoons salt**
> **2 teaspoons pepper**
> **3 tablespoons olive oil**
>
> **Basting Sauce (optional):**
> **¼ cup cider vinegar**
> **¾ cup water**

Preheat oven to 375°.

Press boned leg of lamb open. Rub inside with olive oil. Mix parsley, garlic, sage, rosemary, salt and pepper together. Spread evenly on inside of meat over oil. Roll meat tightly into a circle tucking small end inside roll. Secure with string. Sprinkle outside with salt and pepper.

Place on a rack in a roasting pan. Roast 2 to 3 hours, depending on how you prefer lamb, medium or well. You may want to baste occasionally with vinegar and water mixed together. Basting helps render the fat.

Mr. Steve Stutts

Simply Scampi

Preparation: Easy
Cooking Time: 10 Minutes

Serves: 4

> 1 cup butter
> ¼ cup olive oil
> ¾ teaspoon dried basil
> 1 tablespoon lemon juice
> 1 garlic clove, minced
> ½ teaspoon dried oregano
> 1 tablespoon chopped dried parsley
> Salt and pepper to taste
> 1 to 1½ pounds large fresh shrimp

Preheat oven to 450°.

Melt butter in small saucepan. Combine olive oil, basil, lemon juice, garlic, oregano, parsley, salt and pepper. Add butter. Mix well.

Peel and devein shrimp, leaving tail intact. Butterfly shrimp. Place in a shallow baking dish, shrimp tails up. Pour sauce over shrimp. (Marinate for 30 minutes for additional flavor.)

Bake for 5 minutes. Place under broiler for additional 5 minutes to brown.

Mrs. Richard Sargent
(Ruthann Kerce)

Shrimp Mikanos

*Catch the flavor of the Greek Isles when you serve
this light main course.*

Preparation: Easy   **Serves:** 4
Cooking Time: 1 Hour

3 tablespoons olive oil
2 cups finely chopped onion
1 clove garlic
¼ cup finely chopped parsley
1 tablespoon chopped dill
⅛ teaspoon dry mustard
¼ teaspoon sugar
2 cups chopped tomatoes (fresh
    or canned)
½ cup tomato sauce
1 pound raw shrimp
½ pound Feta cheese, crumbled
Rice (optional)

Preheat oven to 425°.

Heat oil in saucepan and add onion, stirring until onion starts to brown. Add garlic, parsley and dill. Stir in mustard and sugar. Add tomatoes and tomato sauce. Simmer for 30 minutes.

Peel and devein shrimp. Rinse and drain. Add shrimp to sauce and cook briefly. Pour mixture into a 1½ quart casserole and sprinkle with cheese.

Bake 10 to 15 minutes or until cheese is melted. Serve immediately. May be served over rice.

Mrs. Robert Steinbruegge
(Kathy Vogler)

Veal Provençal

Choose your favorite fresh herbs to add your special touch.

Preparation: Somewhat Difficult
Cooking Time: 1 Hour and 30 Minutes

Serves: 6 to 8

2 veal shanks (2 pounds
    each) cut into 6 pieces
    or use veal sirloins on
    the bone (4 pounds)
1 teaspoon salt
1 teaspoon pepper
½ cup flour
½ cup unsalted butter
1 cup chicken broth
1 cup diced carrots
1½ cups diced onions
1 cup chopped leeks
½ cup diced celery
3 cups diced tomatoes

1 teaspoon salt
½ teaspoon pepper
1 cup dry white wine
2 bay leaves
½ teaspoon thyme
2 cloves garlic, crushed
½ cup fresh herbs, chopped
    parsley, chives, basil,
    etc.)
½ teaspoon grated orange
    rind
1 teaspoon grated lemon
    peel

Dredge veal in the flour which has been seasoned with salt and pepper. Brown veal on both sides in the butter for about 7 minutes per side over medium heat. Transfer to a flameproof casserole.

Scrape pan and juices over veal. Add broth. Add carrots, onions, leeks, celery, tomatoes, salt, pepper, wine, bay leaves and thyme. Bring to a boil. Cover and simmer for about 30 minutes.

Add crushed garlic and simmer for another 20 minutes.

Add chopped herbs, orange rind and lemon peel. Cook uncovered for another 25 minutes to reduce juices.

Remove bay leaves and allow dish to stand for at least 30 minutes before serving.

Mrs. Edward W. Hine, Jr.
(Casey Nikoloric)

Veal Raleigh

Attractive dish with a superb taste!

Preparation: Average   **Serves:** 6
Cooking Time: 20 Minutes

> **6 pieces thinly sliced veal**
> **Flour**
> **1 egg, beaten**
> **Bread crumbs**
> **3 tablespoons olive oil**
> **3 tablespoons butter**
> **8 ounces dry vermouth**
> **4 tablespoons butter**
> **Lemon juice**

Dredge veal in flour, dip in beaten egg, then coat with bread crumbs. This can be done up to an hour before cooking.

Heat oil and 3 tablespoons of butter in skillet (copper preferred) and sauté veal until done. Remove veal from skillet and pour off oil and butter. Return skillet to heat and pour in vermouth. Cook until vermouth is reduced by 75 per cent. Stir in remaining butter.

Arrange veal on a serving platter. Drizzle with lemon juice and vermouth sauce. Serve immediately.

Mr. Roy Mann

Sweet and Sour Pot Roast

Deliciously different way to serve roast beef!

Preparation: Easy
Cooking Time: 2 to 3 Hours

2½ pound rump roast or sirloin
   tip roast
1 cup chopped onions
1 clove garlic, minced
¾ cup hot water
1 small bay leaf
2 tablespoons vinegar
1 tablespoon brown sugar
3 tablespoons catsup
¼ cup raisins
¾ teaspoon salt
⅛ teaspoon pepper
1 tablespoon butter or margarine
1½ tablespoons flour

Brown meat in Dutch oven.

Add onions and garlic. Cook until translucent. Add next 8 ingredients and cover and simmer for 2 to 3 hours.

To make gravy, thicken liquid with butter and flour.

Mrs. Edward B. James, Jr.
(Linda Ransom)

Barbecued Ham Slices

Preparation: Easy
Cooking Time: 30 to 45 Minutes

Serves: 6

½ cup orange marmalade
¼ cup prepared mustard
1 teaspoon Worcestershire sauce
¼ cup plus 2 tablespoons water
6 slices fully cooked ham,
about 1 inch thick

Combine first 4 ingredients and mix well. Pour into a large baking dish. Add ham slices, turning to coat. Marinate in refrigerator for about 1 hour.

Remove ham from marinade, reserving marinade for basting.

Place ham 4 or 5 inches from slow to medium coals. Grill for 30 to 45 minutes turning frequently and basting with marinade.

Mrs. David Morgan
(Pam Bagley)

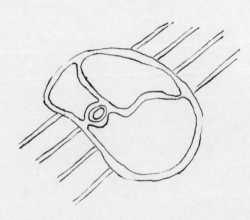

Reuben Casserole

A husband-sized lunch!

Preparation: Easy

Serves: 6

Cooking Time: 15 Minutes

1 (16 ounce) can sauerkraut,
    drained
12 ounces cooked corned beef,
    thinly sliced
2 cups shredded Swiss cheese
½ cup mayonnaise
¼ cup Thousand Island dressing
2 medium tomatoes, sliced
¼ cup rye bread crumbs
1 tablespoon butter

Place sauerkraut in a 1½ quart casserole. Top with corned beef and then cheese. Combine mayonnaise and Thousand Island dressing. Spread over cheese. Top with tomato slices. Set aside.

Place butter in a small glass bowl. Microwave for 1 minute. Stir in bread crumbs. Sprinkle crumb mixture over tomato slices. Microwave for 12 to 14 minutes.

Mrs. Seth L. Knight, Jr.
(Frances Ford)

Marinated Pork Chops

Preparation: Easy (Chill Overnight)
Cooking Time: 30 Minutes

Serves: 6 to 8

> 1 cup soy sauce
> 1 cup salad oil
> ¾ cup lemon juice
> 1 clove garlic, halved
> 6 to 8 thick pork chops,
>   1 to 1½ inches thick

Combine first four ingredients in a small pan. Heat, but do not boil. Pour over pork chops and marinate overnight in refrigerator.

When grilling, baste pork chops with marinade as they cook to keep from drying out.

After grilling, pour marinade sauce over pork chops and warm in the oven to make the meat more tender.

Mrs. William Brewster
(Charla Bargainnier)

Plum Sauce for Roast Lamb

Use over cooked pears for a variation.

Preparation: Easy
Cooking Time: 15 Minutes

Yield: 4 Cups

> 1¼ pounds plums, halved and
>   pitted
> 1½ cups red wine vinegar
> 2 teaspoons ground cloves
> ¾ cup sugar
> 1½ teaspoons dried mint

Combine plums, vinegar, cloves, sugar and mint. Bring to a boil, stir and simmer 15 minutes.

Pour into a processor and purée. Transfer to a bowl. Add more sugar, if desired. Serve warm with lamb.

Apricot Honey Glaze

Excellent for basting with leg of lamb, ham or spareribs.

Preparation: Easy
Cooking Time: 5 Minutes

Yield: 1 Cup

> ½ cup apricot jam or preserves
> ½ cup honey
> 3 tablespoons lemon juice
> ¼ teaspoon cloves
> 1 tablespoon cornstarch

Combine all ingredients in saucepan. Heat, stirring constantly, until sauce is thickened and clear.

Mrs. James McCallie
(Nancy Dague)

Lemon Basting Sauce

Zesty addition to chicken or turkey.

Preparation: Easy
Cooking Time: 10 Minutes

Yield: 2 Cups

¾ cup butter or margarine
2 teaspoons paprika
1 teaspoon sugar
1 teaspoon salt
½ teaspoon black pepper
¼ teaspoon dry mustard
Dash cayenne pepper
½ cup hot water
Several drops Tabasco sauce
½ cup lemon juice

Melt butter in saucepan. Stir in next 6 ingredients. Blend in water, Tabasco and lemon juice.

Use a brush to baste meat in oven or on grill.

Mrs. David Bowen
(Bonnie Risher)

Fourth of July Barbecue Sauce

This family classic makes any cookout a success.
Serve with lamb, beef, pork or chicken.

Preparation: Easy
Cooking Time: 15 Minutes

Yield: 2 Quarts

> 1 pound margarine
> 1 small bottle Worcestershire sauce
> ½ bottle Louisiana hot sauce
> 1½ cups white vinegar
> 3 lemons, juice and sliced rinds
> 1 large onion, sliced
> 1 cup catsup
> 1 tablespoon salt
> 1 tablespoon pepper

Mix all ingredients together in a saucepan. Bring to a boil and boil hard for 5 minutes.

Baste on meat while cooking, then use as a sauce for serving. Keeps 3 to 4 weeks in the refrigerator.

Mr. Arch Farrar, Sr.

Steak Sauce

A homemade sauce that rivals the pros!

Preparation: Easy   **Yield:** 3 Cups
Cooking Time: 45 Minutes

½ cup catsup
1 tablespoon dry mustard
1 medium onion, finely diced
1 cup diced celery
Juice of two lemons
Rind and pulp of one lemon, diced
6 ounces Worcestershire sauce
4 tablespoons liquid smoke
½ teaspoon salt
¼ teaspoon pepper
½ cup butter or margarine

Bring all ingredients, except butter, to a boil and simmer for 45 minutes. Shortly before serving, bring to a boil and add ½ cup of butter or margarine. Serve hot.

Lasts a long time in the refrigerator.

Mr. Charles A. Hight, Sr.

Accompaniments

Accompaniments

Baked Squash
Brussel Sprouts Piquante
Nouvelle Spinach
All American Corn Pudding
Creamed Chestnuts
Baked Potato Casserole
Garden Potato Cups
Golden Cauliflower
Harvest Apple Casserole
Mushrooms Monterey
Rice Verde
Dutch Tomatoes
Spiked Sweet Potatoes

Baked Squash

Water chestnuts give this special flavor and texture.

Preparation: Easy
Cooking Time: 1 Hour and 20 Minutes

Serves: 12

> 2 pounds yellow squash
> 1 onion
> 1 teaspoon salt
> ½ teaspoon white pepper
> 1 pint sour cream
> ½ cup sliced water chestnuts
> 3 eggs, well-beaten
> ¾ cup herb bread dressing
> 3 tablespoons butter

Preheat oven to 350°.

Slice squash and mince onion. Cook in small amount of water until tender. Drain and mash with a fork. Add salt, pepper, sour cream, water chestnuts and eggs. Mix thoroughly.

Butter a 2 quart casserole and sprinkle with half the dressing mixture. Pour in squash mixture and sprinkle with remaining dressing. Dot with butter.

Bake for 1 hour or until knife inserted in center comes out clean.

Mrs. Wallace Grant
(Frances Porter)

Brussel Sprouts Piquante

Enjoyed by even those who are not sprout lovers.

Preparation: Easy   **Serves:** 8 to 10
Cooking Time: 10 Minutes

2 eggs, beaten with fork
¼ cup sugar
½ cup white vinegar
⅓ cup water
1 teaspoon dry mustard
1 teaspoon salt
1 teaspoon pepper
14 bacon strips
1 tablespoon salt
4 (10 ounce) packages frozen
    brussel sprouts, thawed

Combine eggs, sugar, vinegar, water, mustard, 1 teaspoon salt and pepper in a jar. Shake well to mix, then refrigerate.

Before serving, fry bacon until crisp. Remove bacon from pan and pour out all but four tablespoons drippings. Reduce heat to low. Shake refrigerated jar and pour contents into skillet. Stir until thick, then set aside.

Cook sprouts in salted boiling water about 8 minutes and drain.

Serve with warm sauce poured over sprouts. Garnish with crumbled bacon.

Nouvelle Spinach

Great for luncheons. May be prepared, then baked the next day.

Preparation: Average
Cooking Time: 1 Hour and 20 Minutes

Loaf:
- 3 slices bacon
- 4 tablespoons chopped onion
- 1 (10 ounce) package frozen chopped spinach, defrosted or 10 ounces fresh spinach and ¼ cup water
- ¾ cup milk
- 3 tablespoons flour
- 5 medium eggs
- 3 tablespoons cream or milk
- ½ teaspoon salt
- ½ teaspoon pepper
- ½ teaspoon nutmeg
- Cheddar cheese slices

Tomato Sauce:
- 4 large ripe tomatoes, peeled
- ¼ cup catsup
- 1 tablespoon red wine vinegar
- 1 tablespoon oil
- Salt and pepper to taste
- Fresh basil to taste

Loaf:

Preheat oven to 375°.

Grease loaf pan and line with wax paper leaving extra paper on the long sides. Grease paper also.

Fry bacon with onion until brown and crisp. Remove bacon and onion from pan and set aside. Reserve drippings.

Squeeze water out of defrosted spinach into a cup. Add milk to water and set aside.

Add flour to bacon drippings. Whisk and cook until light brown. Add milk mixture gradually, stirring constantly. Bring to a boil. Add spinach, mixing well. Remove from heat.

Mix eggs, cream and seasonings together. Add to spinach mixture. Pour into prepared loaf pan and bake for 50 minutes. Turn off oven and leave in 10 more minutes. Remove from oven. Place cheese slices on top then add crumbled bacon and onion. Return to oven until cheese melts. Serve in slices with fresh tomato sauce.

Tomato Sauce:

Combine all ingredients in processor and serve at room temperature.

Mrs. Scott MacLeod
(Peg Holes)

All American Corn Pudding

Preparation: Easy   **Serves:** 8
Cooking Time: 50 Minutes

> 6 ears fresh corn or
>> 2 (10 ounce) packages frozen
>> corn, defrosted
>
> 2 tablespoons sugar
> 6 tablespoons butter
> 2 tablespoons all-purpose flour
> ½ cup half-and-half
> 4 eggs, well-beaten
> 1½ teaspoons baking powder

Topping:
> 2 tablespoons light brown sugar
> ¼ teaspoon ground cinnamon
> 2 tablespoons butter, melted

Preheat oven to 350°.

Cut corn from ears and set aside.

Melt butter in saucepan and stir in sugar until dissolved. Stir in flour until well-blended. Remove from heat.

Gradually stir in cream. Add eggs and baking powder. Mix well. Stir into corn and pour into buttered 1½ quart soufflé dish. Bake for about 45 minutes or until knife inserted in center comes out clean.

Combine brown sugar and cinnamon. Spread top with melted butter and sprinkle with sugar and cinnamon. Return to oven for an additional 5 minutes.

Mrs. Alfred L. Barron, Jr.
(June Smith)

Creamed Chestnuts

Preparation: Average
Cooking Time: 1 Hour and 10 Minutes

Serves: 6 to 8

> 2 pounds firm chestnuts
>   (may use canned, do not cook)
> 3 tablespoons all-purpose flour
> 3 tablespoons butter
> 2 cups milk
> ½ teaspoon white pepper
> ½ teaspoon salt

Preheat oven to 325°.

Cut an "x" on one side of each chestnut and place on baking sheet. Roast for 45 minutes to one hour. Nuts are ready when skin starts to pull back and meat is tender. Peel nuts.

Make a thick white sauce by first melting butter over medium heat and whisking in flour, dissolving all lumps. Slowly add milk and stir until thick.

Place nuts and sauce in double boiler over medium heat and heat thoroughly.

Mrs. Steve Stutts
(Fielding Hight)

Baked Potato Casserole

Preparation: Easy
Cooking Time: 45 Minutes

Serves: 8

> 6 medium potatoes
> 2 cups shredded sharp cheese
> 4 tablespoons butter
> 2 cups sour cream
> ½ cup chopped chives or green onions
> 6 to 8 slices bacon, cooked, drained
>   and crumbled
> Salt and pepper to taste

Preheat oven to 350°.

Peel and parboil potatoes. Slice and put into a 2½ quart greased casserole. Mix all ingredients and add to potatoes. Stir slightly.

Bake for 30 minutes.

Mrs. William Dismuke, Jr.
(Janice Pursley)

Garden Potato Cups

Low in calories.

Preparation: Average
Cooking Time: 1 Hour and 45 Minutes

Serves: 8

> **4 medium baking potatoes**
> **Vegetable oil**
> **¼ cup butter or margarine**
> **1 small onion, chopped**
> **2 cups shredded cabbage**
> **1 cup grated carrots**
> **½ cup water**
> **⅓ cup chopped green pepper**
> **½ teaspoon salt**
> **⅛ teaspoon white pepper**
> **Carrot curls (optional)**

Preheat oven to 400°.

Wash potatoes and rub with oil. Bake for 1 hour or until done (or bake in microwave).

Melt butter in large skillet. Add onion and sauté until tender. Add cabbage, carrots and water.

Cover and simmer 10 minutes. Stir in green pepper and cook uncovered for an additional 5 minutes or until liquid is absorbed.

Cut potatoes in half lengthwise. Carefully scoop out pulp leaving a ¼ inch shell. Mash pulp and combine with cabbage mixture. Stir in salt and pepper. Stuff shells with mixture.

Bake for 15 minutes.

Garnish with carrot curls if desired.

Mrs. David Morgan
(Pam Bagley)

Golden Cauliflower

A pretty way to serve cauliflower.

Preparation: Easy
Cooking Time: 20 Minutes

Serves: 6

> **1 large head cauliflower**
> **½ cup mayonnaise**
> **2 teaspoons Dijon mustard**
> **¾ cup Cheddar cheese, shredded**

Preheat oven to 350°.

Cook cauliflower in small amount of boiling salted water for about 10 minutes, or until tender. Drain.

Put cauliflower in a one quart casserole. Combine mayonnaise and mustard. Spread on cooked cauliflower. Sprinkle with cheese.

Bake for 10 minutes or until cheese melts.

Mrs. Frank H. Moore, Jr.
(Kiska Medlin)

Harvest Apple Casserole

A "Southern" dish, wonderful with pork or chicken.

Preparation: Easy   **Serves:** 6
Cooking Time: 35 Minutes

2 pounds cooking apples
⅔ cup sugar
1 tablespoon lemon juice
¼ teaspoon ground cinnamon
⅛ teaspoon nutmeg
½ cup sour cream mixed with
    1 tablespoon flour
Sliced almonds and crushed
    macaroons

Preheat oven to 400°.

Peel, core and quarter apples. Cook in small amount of water for approximately 10 to 15 minutes. Drain.

Mix with sugar, lemon juice, cinnamon and nutmeg. Add sour cream and flour last.

Bake for about 20 minutes. Sprinkle with sliced almonds and macaroons for the last five minutes of cooking.

Mrs. Harris Bagley
(Fran Burt)

Mushrooms Monterey

May also be served with toast points as an hors d'oeuvre.

Preparation: Easy
Cooking Time: 20 Minutes

Serves: 6

1 pound mushrooms, sliced
1 tablespoon butter
½ cup sour cream
1 tablespoon flour
¼ teaspoon salt
½ cup grated Parmesan cheese
¼ cup chopped parsley

Preheat oven to 425°.

Sauté mushrooms in butter for about 2 minutes. Blend sour cream, flour, salt and pepper. Stir into mushrooms. Heat until just bubbly. Turn into shallow baking dish. Sprinkle with Parmesan cheese and parsley and bake for 10 minutes.

Mrs. David Morgan
(Pam Bagley)

Rice Verde

Preparation: Easy   **Serves:** 12
Cooking Time: 1 Hour and 5 Minutes

> **2 cups uncooked rice**
> **2 eggs, beaten**
> **⅔ cup vegetable oil**
> **2 cups grated Cheddar cheese**
> **3 medium onions**
> **1 cup parsley**
> **2 green peppers**
> **1 (10½ ounce) can cream of**
>   **mushroom soup**
> **1 clove garlic**
> **2 teaspoons salt**

Preheat oven to 350°.

Put onions, garlic, parsley and green peppers in blender or food processor and process until well-mixed, but not puréed.

Cook rice and mix with other ingredients.

Transfer into buttered oblong dish and bake at 350° for 45 minutes.

Mrs. Armin Maier
(Alden Morris)

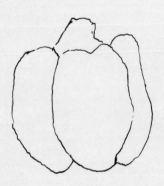

84

Dutch Tomatoes

The sauce enhances this dish.

Preparation: Average
Cooking Time: 20 Minutes

Serves: 6

> 4 to 5 large tomatoes, thickly
>   sliced
> 2 teaspoons salt
> Freshly ground black pepper
> ½ cup flour
> 4 to 6 tablespoons butter
> 2 tablespoons sieved brown sugar
> ¼ teaspoon powdered ginger
> 1 cup heavy cream
> 1 tablespoon finely chopped
>   fresh parsley

Sprinkle tomatoes on both sides with salt and fresh ground black pepper. Dredge tomato slices in flour.

Melt butter over moderate heat in a 12 inch skillet. When foam subsides, add tomato slices and cook for about 5 minutes or until lightly browned.

Mix ginger and brown sugar and sprinkle half over tomatoes. Carefully turn tomatoes over and sprinkle with remaining sugar mixture. Cook 3 to 4 minutes longer, then transfer to a heated serving platter.

Pour cream into pan and boil briskly, stirring constantly, for 2 to 3 minutes or until cream thickens. Season to taste and pour over tomatoes. Sprinkle with chopped parsley.

Mrs. Charles A. Hight, Sr.
(Alberta Booth)

Spiked Sweet Potatoes

This will become a family tradition.

Preparation: Easy   **Serves:** 10 to 12
Cooking Time: 1 Hour and 30 Minutes

> **6 medium sweet potatoes**
> **¼ cup butter**
> **1 cup dark brown sugar, firmly**
>   **packed**
> **½ cup chopped pecans**
> **½ teaspoon cinnamon**
> **½ teaspoon nutmeg**
> **2 tablespoons bourbon**
> **2 eggs, beaten**
> **12 to 15 large marshmallows**

Preheat oven to 300°.

Boil potatoes in their skins until tender (about 45 minutes over medium heat). Drain, run cold water over the potatoes and remove their skins. Beat in an electric mixer or food processor until creamy. Beaters will remove strings from potatoes.

Add remaining ingredients and mix well.

Pour into a 2 quart greased casserole dish and bake for 45 minutes. Place marshmallows on top of potatoes and run under broiler until golden.

Mattie Mae Terhune

Brunches and Breads

Brunches and Breads

Creamy Baked Mushrooms
Berry Coffee Cake
Banana Bread or Muffins
Breakfast Sausage Ring
Danish Puff Pastry
Puffy Omelet
Coffee Break Cake
Tomato Quiche
Mocha Punch
Summer Sangria
Sunday Morning Sweet Rolls
Honey Twist Bread
Cloverleaf Ice Box Rolls
Jalapeño Mexican Hot Bread
Sour Cream Rolls
Whole Wheat Rolls

Creamy Baked Mushrooms

Preparation: Easy
Cooking Time: 40 Minutes

Serves: 4 to 6

> **3 (8 ounce) baskets mushrooms**
> **6 paper thin slices buttered toast**
> **Salt and pepper to taste**
> **1 pint cream**
> **2 teaspoons sherry**
> **Basil (optional)**

Preheat oven to 350°.

Slice mushrooms. Cut crusts off toast and quarter slices.

Place a layer of mushrooms in a buttered casserole. Top with a layer of buttered toast. Salt and pepper. Repeat layers. Basil may be added between layers for a spicier taste.

Pour cream over all and bake 40 minutes. Add sherry just before serving.

Mrs. Edward Hine
(Barbara Brown)

Berry Coffee Cake

Preparation: Average

Cooking Time: 40 Minutes

Serves: 12

> 1 cup sugar
> 1 (8 ounce) package cream cheese,
>   softened
> ½ cup vegetable shortening or
>   margarine
> 2 eggs
> 1 teaspoon vanilla extract
> 1¾ cups all-purpose flour
> 1 teaspoon baking powder
> ½ teaspoon baking soda
> ¼ teaspoon salt
> ¼ cup milk
> ½ cup red raspberry or
>   strawberry preserves
> ½ to ¾ teaspoon ground cinnamon
> ½ cup coarsely chopped pecans

Preheat oven to 350°.

Combine sugar, cream cheese and shortening. Mix until well-blended. Add eggs, one at a time, mixing well after each addition. Blend in vanilla.

Combine dry ingredients. Add alternately to creamed mixture with milk, mixing well after each addition.

Pour mixture into greased and floured 13 x 9 x 2 inch pan or two 9 inch pans. Dot with preserves and sprinkle with cinnamon and chopped pecans. Cut through batter with a knife several times for a marbled effect.

Bake for 35 to 40 minutes.

Mrs. James McCallie
(Nancy Dague)

Banana Bread or Muffins

Butterscotch bits make this wonderfully different.

Preparation: Easy   **Yield:** 1 Loaf or 18 Muffins
Cooking Time: 50 Minutes (Loaf)
                        25 Minutes (Muffins)

> 3 tablespoons butter or margarine
> 1 cup sugar
> 1 egg, beaten
> ½ cup sour cream
> 2 cups all-purpose flour
> 2 teaspoons baking powder
> 1 teaspoon baking soda
> ½ teaspoon salt
> ¾ cup mashed ripe bananas
> 1 tablespoon lemon juice
> 1 (6 ounce) package butterscotch
>   bits

Preheat oven to 375°.

Cream butter and sugar. Add egg and sour cream. Combine dry ingredients. Add alternately with mashed bananas to creamed mixture. Mix well. Add lemon juice. Fold in butterscotch bits.

Spoon into 8½ x 4½ x 3 inch loaf pan that has been well-greased, floured and lined with wax paper or into muffin tins lined with muffin papers. Bake loaf for 50 minutes or muffins for 25 minutes.

Mrs. William Brewster
(Charla Bargainnier)

Breakfast Sausage Ring

May be made ahead of time and reheated in microwave.

Preparation: Easy　　　　　　　　　　　　　　　　　　　　　**Serves:** 8 to 10
Cooking Time: 1 Hour

> **2 eggs, beaten**
> **½ cup milk**
> **1½ cups saltine crackers, crushed**
> **¼ cup finely chopped onion**
> **1 cup chopped apple**
> **2 pounds mild sausage**
> **(one pound hot sausage may**
> **be substituted for one pound**
> **of mild, depending on taste)**

Preheat oven to 350°.

Mix all of the above ingredients together. Pack into a ring mold. Unmold onto a cookie sheet that has edges to hold grease. Bake for 1 hour. Check occasionally to see if grease needs to be drained.

Note: Can be refrigerated in mold overnight and baked the next morning.

Danish Puff Pastry

A little time consuming, but worth the effort.

Preparation: Average
Cooking Time: 1 Hour

Yield: 12 Slices

Pastry:
- ½ cup butter
  (no substitute)
- 1 cup flour
- 2 tablespoons ice water

Puff Mixture:
- ½ cup margarine
- 1 cup water
- 1 teaspoon almond flavoring
- 1 cup all-purpose flour
- Dash salt
- 3 eggs at room
  temperature

Frosting:
- 1½ cups powdered sugar
- ¼ cup butter, softened
  (no substitute)
- 3 to 4 tablespoons milk
- ½ teaspoon almond flavoring
- ½ teaspoon vanilla extract
- ¼ cup toasted almonds or
  pecans

Preheat oven to 350°.

Pastry:
Cut butter into flour. Sprinkle with ice water and mix with a fork. Round into a ball and chill. After chilling, divide dough into 2 equal parts. Stretch and pat into rectangles on ungreased cookie sheet until each piece measures 12 by 3 inches. Rectangles should be 3 inches apart.

Puff Mixture:
Bring margarine and water to a boil. Remove from heat and add almond flavoring and flour that has been sprinkled with salt. Stir with a wooden spoon until well-blended. When smooth and thick, add eggs one at a time. Beat after each addition until batter is smooth and glossy. Divide and place on pastry strips spreading to edges.

Bake for 1 hour. Allow to cool.

Frosting:
Combine sugar, butter, milk and flavorings. Stir until mixture is smooth. Frost cooled puff mixture and sprinkle with nuts.

Linda Mitchell Gholston

Puffy Omelet

Preparation: Average
Cooking Time: 20 Minutes

Serves: 2 to 4

Omelet:
- 6 egg whites at room temperature
- 6 egg yolks
- ¼ teaspoon cream of tartar
- ¾ teaspoon salt
- ½ teaspoon dry mustard
- Dash pepper
- ⅓ cup milk
- 2 teaspoons corn oil
- 2 tablespoons butter

Cheese Sauce:
- 2 tablespoons butter
- 2 tablespoons all-purpose flour
- ½ teaspoon dry mustard
- ¾ teaspoon salt
- Dash pepper
- Dash cayenne pepper
- 1 cup milk
- 1 cup grated sharp Cheddar cheese

Preheat oven to 350°.

Omelet:

Beat egg whites with cream of tartar until very stiff. Set aside. In another bowl beat yolks until thick and lemon colored. Add salt, mustard and pepper. Gradually add milk and beat until well-blended. Fold whites into yolk mixture.

Preheat a 10 inch skillet with a heat resistant handle. Heat oil and butter to sizzling in it, but do not brown. Tilt to coat sides. Spread egg mixture in skillet and cook over low heat about 2 minutes or until underside is firm. Transfer skillet to oven and bake uncovered for 15 minutes or until golden brown and top is firm.

Cheese Sauce:

Make cheese sauce while omelet is in oven. Melt butter and remove from heat. Stir in flour, mustard, salt, pepper, cayenne and milk until smooth. Bring to a boil and stir until thick. Reduce heat and add cheese. Cook, stirring until cheese is melted and mixture is smooth.

When omelet is cooked, take a knife and cut a 1 inch deep ridge right of center. Fold smaller part over larger part. Turn out on platter and spoon sauce over it.

Note: This recipe is even better when filled with bacon, ham or your favorite filling. Simply place on half of omelet before folding.

Mrs. Lynn Dempsey
(Katie Montgomery)

Coffee Break Cake

Preparation: Easy
Cooking Time: 40 Minutes

Serves: 12 to 16

Cake:
½ cup butter or margarine
1 cup sugar
2 eggs
2 cups all-purpose flour
1 teaspoon baking soda
1 teaspoon baking powder
½ teaspoon salt
1 cup sour cream
1 teaspoon vanilla extract

Topping:
⅓ cup brown sugar
¼ cup white sugar
1 teaspoon cinnamon
¼ cup chopped nuts

Preheat oven to 325°.

Cream butter and sugar until light and fluffy. Add eggs one at a time and beat well. Sift dry ingredients together and add alternating with sour cream and vanilla.

Combine all ingredients for topping and stir until well-mixed.

Pour half of batter into well-greased angel food, 9 x 13 inch, or bundt pan. Cover with half of topping. Repeat. Bake for 40 minutes.

Allow to cool for 15 minutes and remove from pan. May be sprinkled with additional cinnamon sugar and nuts.

Mrs. Michael A. Phillips
(Boyce Aldridge)

Tomato Quiche

Especially good with summer tomatoes.

Preparation: Average   **Serves:** 4 to 6
Cooking Time: 1 Hour and 10 Minutes

> 1 medium onion, chopped
> 2 tomatoes, peeled, seeded and
>   chopped
> 2 tablespoons margarine
> ½ teaspoon salt
> ¼ teaspoon thyme
> 9 inch deep dish pie crust
> 8 ounces Swiss cheese, diced
> 2 eggs, beaten
> ⅔ cup half-and-half

Preheat oven to 400°.

Combine onions and tomatoes in a saucepan over medium heat. Add margarine, salt and thyme. Cook until mixture is reduced by half, about 15 to 20 minutes.

Prick pie crust and bake 5 minutes at 400°. Remove from oven and increase oven temperature to 425°.

Line bottom of pie shell with diced Swiss cheese. Pour tomato mixture over the cheese. Mix eggs and half-and-half together and pour into pie shell.

Bake for 10 minutes at 425° then reduce heat to 375° for 35 minutes. Cool 10 minutes before serving.

Mrs. William Dismuke, Jr.
(Janice Pursley)

Mocha Punch

Oh so rich, but oh so good!

Preparation: Easy
Cooking Time: None

Yield: 40 cups

 1 cup instant coffee
 ½ cup cocoa
 1¼ cups sugar
 1 cup boiling water
 3 cups cold water
 2 teaspoons vanilla extract
 3 quarts milk
 1 quart coffee ice cream
 1 quart vanilla ice cream
 1 quart chocolate ice cream
 1 quart whipping cream, whipped
    with 1 cup sugar
 Nutmeg or cinnamon

Combine coffee, cocoa, sugar and boiling water in a large bowl. Add cold water, vanilla and milk. Fold in ice cream just before serving. Ice cream will float. Spread whipped cream on top. Sprinkle with nutmeg or cinnamon.

Mrs. Craig Voss
(Debbie Hulten)

Summer Sangria

Preparation: Easy
Cooking Time: None

Serves: 10 to 15

 1 lemon
 1 lime
 1 orange
 1 (1 pint) basket strawberries,
    washed, hulled and halved
 1 gallon domestic Chablis
 Sugar to taste
 1 quart soda water
 8 to 10 sprigs fresh mint

Squeeze juice from lemon, lime and orange. Slice rinds and set aside.

Mix fruit juices with Chablis. Add strawberries and sliced rinds. Sugar to taste. Stir well and refrigerate until ready to serve. (May be prepared two hours in advance.)

To serve, add soda water, pour over ice and add a sprig of mint.

Mrs. William A. Banks
(Mary Sib Mooney)

Sunday Morning Sweet Rolls

These little wonders can be frozen before adding glaze.

Preparation: Somewhat Difficult (Two Days)
Cooking Time: 10 to 12 Minutes

Yield: 2½ Dozen

Dough:
1 cup sour cream
½ cup butter, melted
½ cup sugar
1 teaspoon salt
2 packages dry yeast
½ cup warm water
    (105° to 115°)
2 eggs, beaten
4 cups all-purpose flour

Filling:
2 (8 ounce) packages cream
    cheese, softened
¾ cup sugar
1 egg
2 teaspoons vanilla extract
¼ teaspoon salt

Glaze:
2 cups powdered sugar
4 tablespoons milk
2 teaspoons vanilla extract

First Day:

Heat sour cream over low heat. Stir in butter, sugar and salt. Cool to lukewarm.

Sprinkle yeast over warm water in a large mixing bowl, stirring until yeast dissolves. Add sour cream mixture to yeast mixture. Next add eggs and flour, gradually stirring well by hand.

Cover tightly. Refrigerate overnight.

Second Day:

Preheat oven to 375°.

Mix filling ingredients together. Blend well and set aside.

Divide dough into four equal parts. Turn onto floured surface and knead each piece 4 or 5 times. Roll each piece into a 12 x 18 inch rectangle.

Spread ¼ of cream cheese filling mixture over each rectangle leaving a ½ inch margin around edge. Carefully roll up jelly roll fashion beginning at long side. Pinch edges and ends to seal. Cut into 1½ inch slices.

Place slices cut side down, 2 inches apart on greased baking sheet. Cover and let rise in a warm place (85°) about 1½ hours or until doubled in size.

Bake 10 to 12 minutes. Do not overcook. They almost have an undercooked look. Filling appears soft.

Mix together glaze ingredients and drizzle over rolls while still warm.

Mrs. Michael S. Williams
(Connie Dingler)

Mrs. Harry Foss
(Karen Davis)

Honey Twist Bread

An easy bread with a wonderful honey crust.

Preparation: Average   **Yield:** 2 Loaves
Cooking Time: 25 to 35 Minutes

Bread:
- 1 cup milk, scalded
- ¼ cup butter
- ½ cup sugar
- 1 teaspoon salt
- 2 cakes yeast
- ¼ cup warm water
   (105° to 115°)
- 2 eggs, well-beaten
- 5 to 6 cups sifted all-purpose
   flour

Honey Topping:
- ¼ cup butter
- ⅔ cup confectioners'
   sugar
- 1 egg white, unbeaten
- 4 tablespoons or more
   warm honey

Bread:

Pour hot milk over butter, sugar and salt. Stir until dissolved. Crumble yeast into warm water. When milk mixture is lukewarm, add yeast and eggs.

Beat in flour to make a soft dough, then knead on floured board until smooth.

Place in well-greased bowl. Cover and let rise until doubled in bulk. Shape into long roll about one inch in diameter. Coil into well-greased cake pans, beginning coil at edge of pans and covering bottom.

Topping:

Cream all topping ingredients together and brush over twist before last rising.

Let bread rise until doubled (about 1½ to 2 hours) and bake in preheated 375° oven for 25 to 35 minutes.

This freezes well.

Mrs. Doug Meadows
(Nancy Sohosky)

Cloverleaf Ice Box Rolls

These are best served right out of the oven.

Preparation: Easy　　　　　　　　　　　　　　　　**Yield:** 2 Dozen
Cooking Time: 10 to 15 Minutes

> ½ cup butter (no substitute)
> ½ cup sugar
> 1 cup milk
> 1 egg, beaten
> 1 package dry yeast
> ¼ cup warm water (105° to 115°)
> 4½ to 5 cups sifted all-purpose
>　　flour
> 1 teaspoon oil

Cream butter and sugar. Scald milk and pour over creamed mixture. Cool. Add beaten egg.

Sprinkle yeast over ¼ cup warm water and wait until dissolved. Add to mixture.

Add sifted flour to mixture with hands until it does not stick to fingers. Don't add too much. Stop with 5 cups—no more. Rub a little oil over top of dough to keep it soft. Place in refrigerator to cool.

Remove from refrigerator. Grease fingers. Form walnut-sized balls of dough. Place three balls in each greased muffin tin to make cloverleaf rolls. (May form Parkerhouse rolls, if desired.)

Let rise in warm place for about 3 hours.

Bake 10 to 14 minutes in preheated 350° oven. Place pan of hot water in bottom of oven.

Note: Dough may be kept in refrigerator 3 or 4 days.

Mrs. Scott MacLeod
(Peg Holes)

Jalapeño Mexican Hot Bread

Outstanding with chili or vegetable soup on a cold day!

Preparation: Easy
Cooking Time: 40 Minutes

Serves: 10 to 12

1½ cups cornmeal
½ cup salad oil
1 cup cream style corn
1 cup buttermilk
3 teaspoons baking powder
1 teaspoon salt
2 eggs
2 Jalapeño peppers or
    ½ (7½ ounce) can Jalapeño
    relish
½ cup chopped onion
1 cup grated Cheddar cheese

Preheat oven to 350°.

Mix together all ingredients except cheese. Pour one half of batter into a very hot greased 10½ inch iron skillet or 8 x 8 inch square pan. Sprinkle in one half of the grated cheese and pour remaining batter and last half of cheese on top.

Bake for 40 minutes.

Note: May use self-rising cornmeal, omitting baking powder and salt.

Mrs. James C. Wyatt
(Betsy Eldridge)

102

Sour Cream Rolls

Pass the butter, please!

Preparation: Easy (Two Days)　　　　　　　　　　　**Yield:** 4 Dozen
Cooking Time: 10 Minutes

½ cup butter or margarine
1 (8 ounce) carton sour cream
½ cup sugar
2 packages dry yeast
½ cup warm water (105° to 115°)
2 eggs, beaten
4 cups all-purpose flour
1 teaspoon salt
Melted butter or margarine

Place ½ cup butter in small saucepan and bring to a boil. Be careful not to brown. Remove from heat and stir in sour cream and sugar. Allow to cool to lukewarm.

Shake yeast over warm water and let sit until completely dissolved in a large mixing bowl. Stir in sour cream mixture and eggs. Combine flour and salt. Gradually, add to yeast mixture, mixing well. Cover and refrigerate overnight.

Punch dough down and divide into 4 equal parts. Roll each into a 10 inch circle on a floured surface. Brush with melted butter. Cut each circle into 12 wedges. Roll up each wedge, beginning at wide end. Place on greased baking sheets. (Cover and let rise in a warm place (85°) until doubled in bulk (about 1 hour).

When ready to bake, preheat oven to 375°. Bake rolls for 10 to 12 minutes or until golden brown.

Mrs. Robert Cates
(Martha Talley)

Whole Wheat Rolls

Light and easy, even for those scared of yeast recipes.

Preparation: Easy   **Yield:** 2 Dozen
Cooking Time: 10 to 12 Minutes

> 1 cup milk
> ¼ cup sugar
> 1 teaspoon salt
> ¼ cup shortening
> 1 package yeast
> ¼ cup warm water (105° to 115°)
> 1 egg
> 2 cups whole wheat flour
> 1½ cups all-purpose flour
> 2 tablespoons butter, melted

Scald milk. Remove from heat and stir in sugar, salt and shortening. Cool to lukewarm.

Sprinkle yeast in warm water and stir until yeast dissolves. Combine milk mixture and yeast mixture.

Add egg and whole wheat flour to yeast mixture, beating until smooth. Add all-purpose flour to make a soft dough. Place dough in a greased bowl, turning dough to grease top of mixture. Cover and let rise in a warm place 1½ to 2 hours (or until doubled).

Punch down and turn out on a lightly floured board. Roll one-half of the dough into a circle (10 inch diameter about ¼ inch thick). Cut into 12 wedges and brush with the melted butter. Roll each wedge tightly (beginning at widest end and rolling toward point) and pinch corners.

Place on lightly greased baking sheets. Cover and let rise 45 minutes or until doubled. Bake in a preheated 400° oven about 10 to 12 minutes or until browned.

Mrs. M. Dwayne Collier
(Jane Gray Cunningham)

Desserts

Desserts

Frozen Almond Ring with Raspberries
Amaretto Cheesecake
Biscuit Tortoni
Black Forest Crêpes
Glazed Praline Cake
Chocolate Bavarian Cream with Almonds
Chocolate Nut Torte
Cocoa Cream Shortcake
Fudge Brownie Pie
Coffee Liqueur Delight
Dacquoise Elegante
Saucy Apple Cake
Snow White Coconut Cake
Fresh Apple Cake
Lemon Ice Cream with Raspberry Sauce
Butterscotch Cake
No-Bake Fruitcake
Tailgate Chocolate Cake
Roulade au Chocolate
Tipsy Pudding

Frozen Almond Ring with Raspberries

Preparation: Average   **Serves:** 6
Cooking Time: None

> **8 ounces whole blanched almonds**
> **½ cup plus 4 tablespoons sugar**
> **½ teaspoon almond extract**
> **4 tablespoons Kirsch**
> **2½ cups whipping cream, divided**
> **1 (10 ounce) package frozen raspberries,**
>   **thawed**

In a food processor or blender grind almonds with ½ cup sugar until fine. Add ½ cup cream, almond extract and Kirsch. Process until puréed. Strain mixture through fine sieve to remove any large particles.

Whip 1 cup of the remaining cream with 2 tablespoons sugar until stiff peaks are formed. Fold into almond mixture. Pour into a 3 cup ring mold and freeze.

Purée raspberries in a food processor or blender, strain and chill. Whip the remaining cup of cream with 2 tablespoons sugar and chill.

When ready to serve, unmold ring by dipping in hot water for several seconds. Spoon some of the raspberry sauce around, but not on it. (The almond ring should remain white.)

To serve, slice mold and add remaining sauce and whipped cream.

Mrs. Robert Weed
(Inge Almanstoetter)

Amaretto Cheesecake

Better when made the day before.

Preparation: Average   **Serves:** 10 to 14
Cooking Time: 2 Hours and 15 Minutes

Crust:
2½ cups graham cracker crumbs
¼ cup sugar
½ cup butter, softened

Filling:
5 (8 ounce) packages cream cheese
1 cup sugar
5 eggs
2 egg yolks
3 tablespoons all-purpose flour
1 tablespoon grated lemon rind
1 cup sour cream
½ cup Amaretto

Topping:
3 ounces sliced almonds
⅓ cup Amaretto

Preheat oven to 475°.

Combine graham crackers, sugar and butter until well-mixed. Press into a 10½ inch spring-form pan, building up sides. Bake for 5 minutes. Refrigerate until ready to use.

Soften cream cheese to room temperature in a large mixing bowl. Beat until creamy. Add sugar and continue to beat. Add eggs and egg yolks one at a time and beat well after each. Sprinkle flour over mixture and add lemon rind. Beat well. Stir in sour cream and Amaretto.

Pour mixture into cooled crust and bake at 475° for 12 minutes. Reduce heat to 250° and bake for 1½ hours. Turn off oven and leave cake in oven with door slightly open for 30 minutes. Remove from oven and cool completely.

After cake has cooled, sprinkle with almonds and pour Amaretto over top. For variety, try substituting sour cream for Amaretto on top of cake.

Mrs. William Dismuke, Jr.
(Janice Pursley)

Biscuit Tortoni

A light frozen dessert.

Preparation: Easy
Cooking Time: None

½ cup toasted almonds
¼ cup sugar
½ cup crushed coconut macaroons
2 ounces milk chocolate, grated
1 (6 ounce) jar maraschino cherries,
    drained and chopped
1 teaspoon grated orange rind
2 cups whipping cream
3 tablespoons confectioners' sugar
1 teaspoon almond extract

In food processor, combine toasted almonds and ¼ cup sugar. Process until very fine. Set aside.

Combine macaroons and almonds. Add chocolate, cherries and orange rind.

Whip cream until soft peaks form. Add confectioners' sugar and almond extract. Fold into almond mixture.

Put into individual paper-lined muffin tins. Freeze until firm.

Mrs. William Byington
(Kathy Leary)

Black Forest Crêpes

These look beautiful and are simple!

Preparation: Average
Cooking Time: 1 Hour

Serves: 10

Crêpes:
- 4 eggs
- ¼ teaspoon salt
- 2 cups all-purpose flour
- 2¼ cups milk
- ¼ cup butter, melted

Sauce:
- 2 (17 ounce) cans dark, sweet pitted cherries
- 1¼ cups powdered sugar
- 2½ tablespoons cornstarch
- ½ cup Amaretto

- ½ gallon vanilla ice cream
- 1 (1 ounce) square semi-sweet chocolate, shaved

Crêpes:

Combine all ingredients in blender and blend for 60 seconds. Turn blender off, scrape down sides and blend another 15 seconds. Chill for at least one hour in refrigerator. If batter appears too thin, add 1 or 2 tablespoons more flour to batter. Blend on low speed and return to refrigerator before using.

When ready to cook, place 2 tablespoons batter in a hot crêpe pan that has been greased. (A non-stick frying pan may be used. Wipe with oil, then heat to medium high.) Tilt pan quickly in all directions to form a round crêpe. Brown lightly on both sides. Makes about 20 crêpes.

Sauce:

Drain cherries, saving ¾ cup juice. Combine sugar and cornstarch in saucepan and stir in Amaretto and cherry juice. Add drained cherries and cook over moderate heat, stirring constantly until slightly thickened.

When ready to serve, scoop ice cream into crêpes. Fold over crêpes and spoon cherry sauce on top. Sprinkle with shaved chocolate.

Mrs. Tim Wallis
(Cathy Clough)

Glazed Praline Cake

Preparation: Average
Cooking Time: 1 Hour and 15 Minutes

Serves: 16

Cake:
- 1 cup butter
- ½ cup shortening
- 16 ounces light brown sugar
- 1 cup white sugar
- 5 eggs
- 3 cups sifted all-purpose flour
- ½ teaspoon salt
- 1 teaspoon baking powder
- 1 cup milk
- 1 teaspoon vanilla extract
- 1 cup chopped walnuts

Walnut Glaze:
- 1 cup confectioners' sugar
- 2 tablespoons butter
- 6 tablespoons half-and-half
- ½ teaspoon vanilla extract
- ½ cup chopped walnuts

Preheat oven to 350°.

In a large bowl, cream butter and shortening together. Gradually add both sugars to butter mixture. Cream until light and fluffy. Beat in eggs one at a time. Set aside.

Sift together flour, salt and baking powder. Set aside. Mix together 1 cup milk and 1 teaspoon vanilla extract. Alternately add the flour mixture and the milk to the sugar mixture. Stir in walnuts. Blend well.

Pour into a large greased and floured tube pan. Bake 1 hour and 15 minutes.

While cake is baking mix glaze ingredients together. Cream confectioners' sugar and butter. Add cream and vanilla, mixing well. Add chopped walnuts, blending thoroughly.

Cool cake 10 minutes then turn out of pan onto a plate. Evenly glaze.

Keep covered in a cool, dry place.

Note: May substitute black walnuts for English walnuts.

Mrs. Raymon H. Cox
(Jeanne Marie Blackburn)

Chocolate Bavarian Cream with Almonds

Preparation: Average   **Serves:** 6 to 8
Cooking Time: 15 Minutes

>   5 egg yolks
>   1 cup sugar, divided
>   1 cup half-and-half
>   4 (1 ounce) squares semi-sweet
>   chocolate
>   1 envelope unflavored gelatin
>   ¾ cup slivered almonds
>   1 cup heavy cream, whipped
>
> **Garnish:**
> **Heavy cream, sweetened and whipped**
> **Whole cherries, 1 per serving**

Combine egg yolks with ½ cup sugar in bowl and beat until light in color and fluffy.

In saucepan, combine half-and-half, chocolate squares and gelatin. Stir over medium heat until gelatin is dissolved and chocolate melts. Gradually beat chocolate mixture into egg mixture. Chill until mixture starts to thicken, stirring occasionally.

In skillet heat remaining ½ cup sugar over medium heat until it is liquid and golden. Quickly add almonds and pour onto buttered cookie sheet. Cool until hard. Crush with rolling pin.

Fold whipped cream into chilled chocolate mixture. Layer almonds and chocolate mixture in individual parfait glasses or champagne glasses. Chill until ready to serve, then garnish with dollop of whipped cream topped with a cherry.

Mrs. Robert Weed
(Inge Almanstoetter)

Chocolate Nut Torte

Very rich! Very elegant!

Preparation: Average
Cooking Time: 45 Minutes

Torte layers:
- 7 eggs, separated
- ¼ teaspoon salt
- 1 cup sugar
- 1 teaspoon vanilla extract
- 1¼ cups combination ground almonds and pecans
- ¼ cup packaged dry bread crumbs
- 1 teaspoon baking powder
- ½ teaspoon salt

Filling:
- 1 cup whipping cream
- ½ cup confectioners' sugar
- 1 teaspoon vanilla extract

Frosting:
- 4 (1 ounce) squares unsweetened chocolate
- ¼ cup butter
- 3 cups sifted confectioners' sugar
- ½ cup hot coffee
- 1½ teaspoons vanilla extract

Decoration:
- 1 cup frosting
- Pecan halves or almond slivers

Preheat oven to 375°.

Separate eggs and place whites in a large bowl, yolks in a small bowl. Let egg whites come to room temperature. Line bottoms of three 8 inch round layer pans with circles of wax paper and grease lightly.

With mixer on high speed beat egg whites until stiff. Add salt and gradually add ½ cup sugar. Beat until stiff peaks form. Beat yolks until thick and light. Gradually beat in the other ½ cup sugar until thick, about three minutes. Beat in vanilla.

Combine ground nuts, bread crumbs, baking powder and salt. Fold this into yolk mixture with rubber spatula. Mix well with under and over motion. Fold this mixture into egg whites until combined.

Divide evenly into three pans, smoothing the tops. Bake 25 minutes at 375°. Cool at least one hour.

Filling:
Pour whipping cream, confectioners' sugar and vanilla into a medium bowl. Beat until stiff and refrigerate.

Frosting:
Melt chocolate and butter over water in a double boiler. Remove from water. Mix in confectioners' sugar, hot coffee and vanilla until smooth.

Cake Assemblage:
Loosen cake layers with a knife and turn out of pans. Remove wax paper. Assemble layers with filling between. Reserve 1 cup of frosting mixture. Frost cake with remaining frosting. Put reserved frosting in a pastry bag fitted with a #2 star tip. Pipe 10 to 12 stars onto top of cake. Place pecan halves or almond slivers on stars to decorate. Refrigerate at least one hour.

Mrs. F. Lynn Dempsey
(Katie Montgomery)

Cocoa Cream Shortcake

The fruit topping makes this cake really scrumptious!

Preparation: Average
Cooking Time: 30 Minutes

Serves: 16

Cake:
- 1 cup (7 or 8) egg whites
- ½ cup sifted or stirred cocoa
- ¾ cup boiling water
- 1¾ cups all-purpose flour
- 1¾ cups sugar
- 1½ teaspoons baking soda
- 1 teaspoon salt
- ½ cup salad oil
- 7 egg yolks
- 2 teaspoons vanilla extract
- ½ teaspoon cream of tartar

Frosting:
- 3 cups whipping cream
- 1 cup confectioners' sugar
- ⅓ cup cocoa
- 1 tablespoon vanilla extract

Fruit Topping:
- 4 cups strawberries, sliced
- ¾ cup sugar
- 2 tablespoons rum
- 1 tablespoon lemon juice

Cake:
Place egg whites in a large bowl and allow to come to room temperature.

Preheat oven to 325°.

Combine cocoa and boiling water and stir until smooth. Allow to cool.

Sift flour, sugar, soda and salt together. Add oil, egg yolks, vanilla and cooled cocoa. Beat until smooth.

Beat egg whites with cream of tartar. Pour yolk mixture over whites and fold in with rubber spatula. Pour into three greased and floured 9 inch cake pans. Bake 30 minutes. Cool before removing from pans.

Frosting:
Combine frosting ingredients and refrigerate for one hour. Remove from refrigerator and beat until stiff. Frost layers and sides of cake. Refrigerate until just before serving.

Topping:
About 30 minutes before serving, mix all topping ingredients together. Refrigerate. When ready to serve, decorate top of cake with half the strawberries, drained. Serve remaining strawberries in juice with cake. Refrigerate any leftover cake.

Mrs. Edward B. James, Jr.
(Linda Ransom)

Fudge Brownie Pie

Great with very little effort.

Preparation: Easy
Cooking Time: 45 Minutes

Serves: 6

½ cup margarine
2 (1 ounce) squares unsweetened
　chocolate
1 cup sugar
½ cup all-purpose flour
2 eggs
½ cup chopped pecans
1 tablespoon vanilla extract

Preheat oven to 325°.

Melt margarine and chocolate together over very low direct heat. Remove from heat and add sugar, then eggs.

Add flour, nuts and vanilla. Mix well.

Pour into a well-buttered glass pie plate. Bake 25 to 30 minutes.

Cut into wedges and serve warm topped with ice cream for an unbeatable flavor.

Note: Cut while warm.

Mrs. Charles F. Jackson, Jr.
(Christa Cline)

Coffee Liqueur Delight

This will bring raves from all of your guests!

Preparation: Easy
Cooking Time: None

Serves: 2 to 4

¼ cup Amaretto
¼ cup Kahlua or Tia Maria
1½ cups vanilla ice cream
5 to 7 ice cubes

Put all ingredients in electric blender and process until frothy. Serve immediately.

Mrs. E. Dean Saville
(Ansley Briley)

Dacquoise Elegante

Truly a culinary experience.

Preparation: Somewhat Difficult   **Serves:** 6 to 8
Cooking Time: 1 Hour 30 Minutes

Meringues:
¾ cup blanched whole almonds,
    without skins
4 egg whites
1 cup sugar
Pinch of cream of tartar
Parchment paper

Filling and Sauce:
¾ cup dried apricots
Strip of lemon rind
1 cup heavy cream, whipped
Sugar to taste
½ cup sugar
¾ cup water
Juice of ½ lemon

Garnish:
2 tablespoons confectioners'
    sugar
½ cup heavy cream, whipped
1 (1 ounce) square semi-sweet
    chocolate, grated

Meringues:
Preheat oven to 275°.

Line 2 baking sheets with parchment paper. Draw an 8 inch circle on each.

Pour boiling water over almonds and soak for 10 minutes before draining, drying and grinding.

Beat egg whites until stiff. Add 1 tablespoon sugar and cream of tartar. Continue beating 1 minute or until mixture is glossy. Fold in remaining sugar and ground almonds.

Spread mixture evenly on parchment circles. Bake 1 hour. To test for doneness, lift a corner of the paper. If paper peels away clearly, the meringues are baked. If not, continue baking 15 minutes longer and test again. When done, remove paper and set aside to cool.

Filling and Sauce:
Soak apricots according to package directions. Simmer gently in soaking liquid, adding lemon rind. When tender, remove rind and purée in food processor. Allow to cool.

116

Stir ⅓ of purée into 1 cup whipped cream. Add sugar to taste.

To make sauce, heat ½ cup sugar and ¾ cup water until dissolved. Add lemon juice and boil 3 minutes. Add remaining apricot purée, stirring well.

To assemble, sandwich the filling between the meringue layers. Sprinkle the top with confectioners' sugar and decorate with rosettes of whipped cream. Top with grated chocolate. Serve with sauce.

Mr. Al Ledbetter

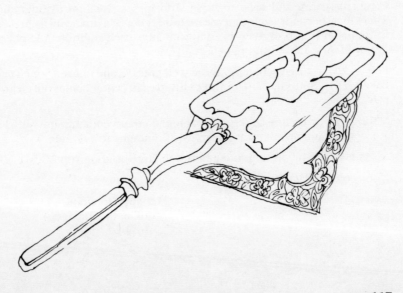

Saucy Apple Cake

Good for those who don't like fruitcake, but want
something extra special during the holidays.

Preparation: Average
Cooking Time: 3 Hours

Serves: 16

Cake:

- 3 cups dried apples
- Sugar to taste
- 1 cup fig preserves
- 1 cup watermelon rind preserves
- 1 cup crystallized cherries (green and red)
- 1 (15 ounce) box white seedless raisins
- 2 cups chopped pecans
- 4 cups all-purpose flour
- 1 cup margarine
- 2 cups sugar
- 1½ teaspoons cinnamon
- 1½ teaspoons ground cloves
- 1 teaspoon ground nutmeg
- 1 teaspoon salt
- 1 teaspoon baking soda

Filling:

- 1 (20 ounce) can crushed pineapple, drained
- 1 grated orange rind
- Juice of 1 orange
- 1 grated lemon rind
- Juice of 2 lemons
- 3 (6 ounce) packages frozen coconut
- ¼ cup margarine
- 2 cups sugar

Preheat oven to 250°.

Stew apples in a small amount of water and sweeten to taste. Cut fig and watermelon rind preserves in small pieces. Flour all nuts, raisins, fruit and preserves using some of the 4 cups flour, placing each ingredient in a separate bowl.

Cream margarine and sugar together. Add apples. Combine dry ingredients and spices together and beat into apple mixture, 1 cup at a time. Add fig preserves and watermelon rind preserves, beating well after each addition. Add cherries and mix well. Add raisins and nuts last.

Pour cake mixture evenly into three well-greased and floured 9 inch cake pans. Bake 1½ to 2 hours or until toothpick inserted in center comes out clean. Cool in pans.

Make filling by mixing all ingredients together and cooking slowly on low heat. Stir constantly until thick and glazed (30 minutes to one hour).

Assemble cake by placing filling between layers and on top of cake.

Note: Keep refrigerated.

Mrs. Jim Hobgood
(LouElla McCarthney)

Snow White Coconut Cake

*During the holidays, try a sprig of holly and berries
on the top to add a festive touch!*

Preparation: Somewhat Difficult (2 Days)　　　　　**Serves:** 14 to 16
Cooking Time: 45 Minutes

Cake:
- 1 cup butter, softened
- ½ cup vegetable shortening
- 3 cups sifted white sugar
- 5 eggs
- 3 cups cake flour (all-purpose flour may be used)
- ½ teaspoon baking powder
- 1 cup milk
- ½ teaspoon vanilla extract
- ½ teaspoon lemon flavoring
- 1 fresh coconut

Icing:
- 4 egg whites
- 3 cups sugar
- 3 teaspoons light corn syrup
- ⅔ cup water
- ¼ teaspoon salt
- ½ teaspoon vanilla extract

First Day:
Preheat oven to 375°.

Cream butter and shortening until very fluffy. Cream with sugar. Add eggs one at a time, mixing thoroughly after each addition. Add baking powder to flour and fold in alternately with milk. Add vanilla extract and lemon flavoring. Bake in 3 well-greased 9 inch cake pans for 30 minutes.

Use a fresh coconut for the coconut milk. Drain all milk from the coconut and strain out any residue. After cake is fully cooled, pierce each layer several times with a toothpick. Pour a scant ¼ cup coconut milk over each layer and let it soak in. Stack layers with wax paper separating each layer and cover tightly with aluminum foil. Store in refrigerator overnight. Grate coconut as fine as possible and store in refrigerator to use with icing.

Second Day:
Icing:
Combine egg whites with remaining ingredients except vanilla in top of double boiler. Beat well with rotary beater and place over boiling water. Cook, beating continuously, until stiff peaks are formed (about 10 minutes). Remove from heat, add vanilla and beat about 2 minutes more. Makes enough frosting to generously frost cake with frosting between layers and on top. After the cake is frosted, throw grated coconut on top and sides of cake. This will give the cake a fluffy appearance. Do not press the coconut into the icing.

Mrs. David A. Hall
(Patti Jones)

119

Fresh Apple Cake

Old-fashioned good!

Preparation: Average
Cooking Time: 55 Minutes

Serves: 10 to 12

Cake:
- 1½ cups oil
- 2 cups sugar
- 3 eggs
- 2 teaspoons vanilla extract
- 2½ cups sifted all-purpose flour
- 1 teaspoon salt
- 1 teaspoon baking soda
- 2 teaspoons cinnamon
- 2 teaspoons baking powder
- 2 teaspoons allspice
- 1 cup chopped pecans
- 3 cups chopped apples

Topping:
- 1 cup confectioners' sugar
- Juice and grated rind of 1 lemon
- ⅛ stick butter, melted

Preheat oven to 350°.

Blend oil, sugar, eggs and vanilla in mixing bowl. Sift dry ingredients together and add to egg mixture. Fold in pecans and apples.

Pour into a greased and floured bundt pan. Bake for 55 minutes.

Remove pan from oven and let cool 15 minutes. Remove cake from pan.

Combine topping ingredients and pour over warm cake. May be served with a dab of whipped cream on top.

Mrs. Charles Betz
(Brenda Sermersheim)

Lemon Ice Cream with Raspberry Sauce

Refreshing and light!

Preparation: Easy
Cooking Time: 10 Minutes

Yield: 1 Gallon

Ice Cream:
1 quart whipping cream
1 quart whole milk
Juice of 6 lemons
3 cups sugar
2 teaspoons lemon extract
1 tablespoon grated lemon
    rind

Sauce:
1 (16 ounce) package frozen
    raspberries
1 teaspoon cornstarch
¼ cup sugar
4 tablespoons Cointreau
1 tablespoon water
½ cup red currant jelly
Mint leaves for garnish
    (optional)

Mix ice cream ingredients together thoroughly. Pour into ice cream freezer can. Freeze according to manufacturer's instructions.

Sauce:
Thaw raspberries. Warm in small saucepan and strain. Return berries to pan. Mix cornstarch with water and add to strained berries. Simmer 5 minutes over medium heat.

Add sugar and jelly to berries. Stir until sugar is dissolved. Add Cointreau. Cool.

Spoon sauce around sides of a scoop of ice cream. Garnish with a mint leaf.

Mrs. John Kirkland
(Mary Kaebnick)

Butterscotch Cake

A great cake for any special occasion.

Preparation: Somewhat Difficult
Cooking Time: 1 Hour

Serves: 12

Cake:
- ⅔ cup butterscotch morsels
- ¼ cup water
- 2¼ cups all-purpose flour
- 1 teaspoon salt
- 1 teaspoon baking soda
- ½ teaspoon baking powder
- 1¼ cups sugar
- ½ cup shortening
- 3 eggs, unbeaten
- 1 cup buttermilk

Filling:
- ½ cup sugar
- 1 tablespoon cornstarch
- ½ cup evaporated milk
- ⅓ cup water
- ⅓ cup butterscotch morsels
- 1 egg yolk, beaten
- 2 tablespoons butter
- 1 cup coconut
- 1 cup chopped nuts

Sea Foam Frosting:
- ⅓ cup white sugar
- ⅓ cup brown sugar
- ⅓ cup water
- 1 tablespoon corn syrup
- 1 egg white
- ¼ teaspoon cream of tartar

Cake:
Preheat oven to 375°.

Combine morsels and water in saucepan. Cook on medium heat until morsels are melted. Set aside and allow to cool.

Sift dry ingredients together and set aside.

In large bowl cream sugar and shortening. Blend in eggs and cooled butterscotch morsels. Mix well.

Add dry ingredients alternately with buttermilk beginning and ending with dry ingredients.

Pour into 2 greased and lined 9 inch round cake pans. Bake for 25 to 30 minutes. Cool.

Filling:
Combine first 6 ingredients in saucepan. Cook over medium heat stirring constantly until thick. Remove from heat. Add butter, coconut and nuts. Spread half of filling between 2 cake layers and other half on top layer.

Sea Foam Frosting:
Combine first 4 ingredients in saucepan cooking without stirring until syrup reaches soft ball stage (235°-240° on candy thermometer). Beat egg white with cream of tartar until stiff peaks form. Add syrup to egg white in slow stream, beating until thick. Spread on sides of cake and one inch circumference on edge of top layer.

Mrs. Raymon H. Cox
(Jeanne Marie Blackburn)

No-Bake Fruitcake

Preparation: Easy (Chill Overnight)
Cooking Time: 45 Minutes

Serves: 24

> 1 pound marshmallows
> ¾ cup milk
> 1 pound graham crackers
> 1 (15 ounce) box seedless raisins
> 1 pint mixed candied fruit
> 1 cup candied cherries
> 4 cups nuts

Combine marshmallows and milk in top of double boiler. Place over simmering water until marshmallows melt.

Crush graham crackers in blender or food processor until fine. Mix with fruit and nuts, using hands.

Pour melted marshmallow mixture over this and mix well with hands.

Line an angel food pan with wax paper and press cake into it. Pack tightly. (Wet hands to keep mixture from being sticky.) Cover and refrigerate for 24 hours.

Turn cake out next day and garnish with pecan and cherry halves. Wrap in tea towel and keep refrigerated.

Note: This freezes beautifully or will keep in the refrigerator for two weeks.

Pat Hensley Lake

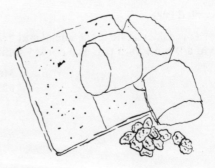

Tailgate Chocolate Cake

An easy dessert to serve a crowd.

Preparation: Easy
Cooking Time: 20 to 25 Minutes

Serves: 25 to 30

Cake:
- 2 cups all-purpose flour
- 2 cups sugar
- ½ teaspoon salt
- ½ cup butter
- ½ cup cooking oil
- 3 tablespoons cocoa
- 1 cup water
- 2 eggs, well-beaten
- 1 teaspoon baking soda
- ½ cup buttermilk
- 1 teaspoon vanilla extract
- ½ teaspoon almond flavoring

Icing:
- 6 tablespoons milk
- ½ cup butter
- 3 tablespoons cocoa
- 1 (16 ounce) box confectioners' sugar
- 1 teaspoon vanilla extract
- 1 cup chopped nuts (optional)

Preheat oven to 350°.

Mix flour, sugar and salt together and set aside.

In a saucepan mix butter, cooking oil, cocoa and water. Bring to a boil, stirring constantly, and pour over the flour and sugar mixture.

In a small bowl, combine well-beaten eggs, soda, buttermilk and flavorings.

Combine all ingredients and pour into an 18 x 20 inch pan which has been prepared with shortening or margarine and floured.

Bake for 20 to 25 minutes or until center springs back to the touch. (Do not use straw test with this cake.)

Icing:
Combine milk, butter and cocoa in a small saucepan. Stir over medium heat until well-blended.

Pour warmed ingredients over the confectioners' sugar. Add vanilla and nuts.

Ice cooled cake.

Note: This cake can be made ahead and frozen if necessary. For a thicker cake, bake in a 9 x 13 inch pan and cook 5 minutes longer. Serves 15.

Mrs. Robert Payne
(Mary Louise Diden)

Roulade au Chocolate

Preparation: Average
Cooking Time: 25 Minutes

Serves: 12

**1 (6 ounce) package semi-sweet
    chocolate morsels**
**2 tablespoons plus 1 teaspoon
    strong black coffee (brewed)**
5 eggs
1¼ cups sugar, divided
1 teaspoon vanilla extract
2 teaspoons cocoa
1 cup whipping cream
2 tablespoons confectioners' sugar
3 tablespoons coffee-flavored liqueur
Chocolate curls

Preheat oven to 350°.

Separate eggs, allowing yolks and whites to come to room temperature.

Grease bottom and sides of a 15 x 10 x 1 inch jelly roll pan with vegetable oil, line with wax paper and grease paper also.

In top of double boiler, heat chocolate morsels and coffee, bringing water to a boil. Reduce heat to low. Stir occasionally until chocolate melts.

Place egg yolks in a large bowl, beating at high speed of mixer until foamy. Add ¾ cup sugar gradually. Continue beating until mixture is lemon-colored and thick. Slowly stir portion of hot chocolate mixture into yolk mixture (so that yolks do not cook). Fold in the rest of the chocolate mixture.

Using mixer, beat egg whites on high speed until foamy. Add ½ cup sugar slowly, beating until stiff peaks form. Fold egg whites into chocolate mixture. Fold in vanilla extract.

Pour chocolate mixture into pan and bake on center rack of oven for 15 to 18 minutes. Be careful not to overcook. Cover top with damp linen towel (or damp paper towels). Let cool on wire rack for approximately 20 minutes. Gently remove towel and run knife around edges of cake, loosening gently. Sift cocoa over entire top of cake.

To remove cake from pan, place two (18 inch) lengths of wax paper on a slightly damp surface. Invert cake onto wax paper, removing the pan and peeling paper from cake.

Filling: Beat whipping cream until foamy, slowly add 2 tablespoons confectioners' sugar and liqueur, continue to beat until soft peaks form.

Spread whipped cream over cake leaving a 1 inch margin on all sides. (Reserve small amount of whipped cream to garnish top of roulade.) With long side facing you, carefully roll the cake, using the wax paper as support. Gently transfer roulade to large serving plate.

Pipe reserved whipped cream across top of roulade and garnish with chocolate curls. Refrigerate until ready to serve.

Mrs. Robert N. Farrar
(Susan Gates)

Tipsy Pudding

Great bourbony taste!

Preparation: Easy
Cooking Time: 35 Minutes

Serves: 6 to 8

Pudding:
1 cup chopped pecans
1 cup golden raisins
1 cup dark brown sugar
¾ cup light corn syrup
4 eggs
¼ cup bourbon
¼ cup butter, melted
1 teaspoon vanilla extract
½ teaspoon salt
½ cup pecan halves

Topping:
1 cup whipping cream
2 tablespoons bourbon
1 tablespoon sugar

Place rack in center of oven and preheat to 400°.

Butter a 9 inch glass pie plate. Sprinkle plate with chopped pecans and raisins.

Combine sugar, corn syrup, eggs, bourbon, butter, vanilla and salt. Mix well and pour over nuts and raisins. Arrange pecan halves on top.

Bake 10 minutes at 400°, then reduce heat to 325° and bake 25 minutes until set.

Whip topping ingredients together until soft peaks form. Slice pudding into wedges and serve warm with a dollop of topping.

Mrs. Steve Stutts
(Fielding Hight)

Gifts

Mexican Hot Sauce
Butterscotch Pecan Cookies
Christmas Fudge
Cinnamon Pecan Fingers
Angelic Divinity
Country Store Soft Ginger Cookies
Maple Butterscotch Sauce
Creole Pralines
Fruitcake Cookies
Chocolate Cups
Microwave Pecan Brittle
Apricot Bars
Graham Cracker House

Mexican Hot Sauce

Preparation: Easy

Yield: 16 (½ Pint) Jars

Cooking Time: 4 Hours

> 2 gallons fresh ripe tomatoes,
>   skinned or 2 (1 gallon) cans
>   tomatoes
> 5 large onions, coarsely chopped
> ½ pound finely chopped Jalapeño
>   peppers (fresh)
> 1 cup white vinegar
> ½ to ⅔ cup sugar to taste
> Salt to taste

Combine all ingredients in a large pot (be careful not to get it too sweet!) and cook until it thickens. This will take 3 to 4 hours, stirring occasionally.

While sauce is still hot, pour into Mason jars which have been washed and scalded. Cover with new canning lids and rings and leave on counter until cooled. As it cools, the lids will pop which means they are sealing.

The jars should not be disturbed until they are cool or the seal may be broken. These can be stored on the shelf for months.

Serve with tortilla chips as a dip or as a condiment.

Mrs. Leon Sproles
(Susan Scott)

Butterscotch Pecan Cookies

A family recipe that has been passed down for generations. Fun to make with children.

Preparation: Average (Chill Overnight)   **Yield:** 6 Dozen
Cooking Time: 8 to 10 Minutes

> 4 cups sifted all-purpose flour
> 1 teaspoon baking soda
> ½ teaspoon salt
> 1 tablespoon cream of tartar
> 1 cup butter or margarine
> 2 cups brown sugar
> 2 eggs
> 1 teaspoon vanilla extract
> 1 cup chopped pecans

Sift together flour, soda, salt and cream of tartar. Set aside. Cream butter or margarine and sugar until light and fluffy. Add eggs and vanilla. Beat well. Add flour mixture to creamed mixture. Add pecans and mix well. Shape into rolls and wrap in wax paper. Chill overnight.

When ready to bake, preheat oven to 400°. Slice cookies and bake on ungreased baking sheet for 8 to 10 minutes.

Dough can be frozen.

Mrs. William R. Vogler
(Lynn Rubio)

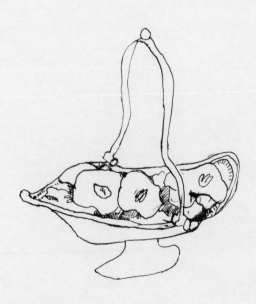

Christmas Fudge

A chocoholic's fantasy!

Preparation: Average
Cooking Time: 10 Minutes

Yield: 8 Dozen (1 Inch Squares)

2 (12 ounce) packages semi-sweet
    chocolate morsels
3 ounces milk chocolate bar
1 (7 ounce) jar marshmallow cream
4½ cups sugar
1 teaspoon salt
1 (12 ounce) can evaporated milk
1 ounce bitter baking chocolate,
    grated
2 to 3 cups broken pecans

Combine chocolate morsels, broken milk chocolate bar and marshmallow cream in a large bowl.

Combine sugar, salt, evaporated milk and grated baking chocolate in a large saucepan. Bring to a boil over medium heat, stirring constantly. Boil 4½ minutes.

Add one half of boiled syrup mixture to the ingredients in the bowl and stir. Add nuts to taste. Then add the rest of the boiled syrup and stir until completely mixed.

Pour into a 9 x 13 inch pan greased or lined with foil. Allow to set up about 4 hours before cutting into squares.

Mrs. William Dismuke, Jr.
(Janice Pursley)

Cinnamon Pecan Fingers

A nice little bite.

Preparation: Easy
Cooking Time: 20 to 25 Minutes

Yield: 6 Dozen

¾ cup butter
1 cup sugar
2 teaspoons cinnamon
1 egg, separated
2 cups sifted all-purpose flour
1 cup chopped pecans

Preheat oven to 325°.

Cream butter, sugar and cinnamon together. Add egg yolk and flour.

Knead this mixture well with hands. Press into a 10½ x 15½ inch greased pan.

Glaze top with beaten egg white and spread nuts over top.

Bake for 20 to 25 minutes until light brown.

Cut into fingers before cooling and remove from pan.

Mrs. Harris L. Bagley
(Fran Burt)

Angelic Divinity

Preparation: Average
Cooking Time: 20 Minutes

Yield: 3 Dozen

3 cups sugar
½ cup light corn syrup
¾ cup water
¼ cup egg whites (2 large eggs)
½ teaspoon salt
1 teaspoon vanilla extract
1 cup chopped nuts

Combine sugar, syrup and water in saucepan. Cook over low heat and stir until sugar is dissolved. Increase heat and boil without stirring until candy thermometer reaches 240°. Remove from heat.

Combine egg whites, salt and vanilla. Beat on high speed until stiff, moist peaks form. Do not beat until dry. With mixer on high speed, slowly pour in hot syrup in a thin stream. Beat until mixture holds shape but is still glossy.

Stir in nuts and pour mixture into a buttered pan. Spread evenly. Cut into small squares when cool.

Mrs. Frank Pinson
(Ruth Slickman)

Country Store Soft Ginger Cookies

*Once your family smells these cooking, they won't
let you give them away!*

Preparation: Average   **Yield:** 6 Dozen
Cooking Time: 15 Minutes

> 1 pound unsalted butter
> 3 cups sugar
> 1 cup unsulphured molasses
> 3 large eggs
> 8 cups all-purpose flour
> 1 teaspoon salt
> 1½ tablespoons baking soda
> 1½ tablespoons ginger
> 1 tablespoon ground cloves
> 1 tablespoon ground cinnamon
> Sugar (to roll cookies in)

Preheat oven to 350°.

In a very large bowl, cream butter. Beat in sugar until light and fluffy. Beat in molasses. Add eggs one at a time, beating well after each one.

Sift dry ingredients together. Stir into butter mixture and blend well.

Roll into 1½ inch balls and roll in sugar. Place 2 inches apart on ungreased cookie sheet. Bake for 13 to 15 minutes.

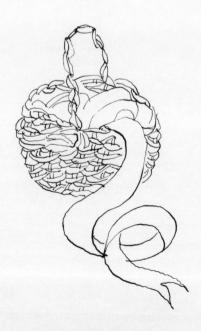

Maple Butterscotch Sauce

Warm someone's heart with a gift that adds that special touch to any dessert.

Preparation: Average
Cooking Time: 15 Minutes

Yield: 1 Cup

¼ **cup butter**
1 **cup brown sugar, firmly packed**
2 **egg yolks, well-beaten**
½ **cup cream**
⅛ **teaspoon salt**
½ **teaspoon maple flavoring**
½ **cup chopped walnuts**

Cream butter thoroughly. Add sugar gradually, beating well. Add egg yolks, cream and salt. Blend well.

Cook in double boiler over boiling water until creamy and thick. Remove from heat and cool slightly.

Add maple flavoring and walnuts.

Serve warm or cooled over ice cream, pudding or cake.

Mrs. William M. Huffman
(Jo Gross)

Creole Pralines

Bet you can't eat just one!

Preparation: Difficult
Cooking Time: 1 Hour

Yield: 5 to 6 Dozen

> **2 cups sugar**
> **1 cup light brown sugar, firmly**
> **packed**
> **½ cup margarine**
> **1 cup evaporated milk**
> **2 tablespoons light corn syrup**
> **1 teaspoon vanilla extract**
> **2 to 2½ cups broken pecans**

Combine first 5 ingredients in a 3 quart saucepan. Bring to a boil and cook 20 to 30 minutes on low heat until it reaches a temperature of 225° on a candy thermometer. Keep it bubbling and stir often.

Once temperature of 225° is reached, add vanilla and pecans and continue to cook for 15 to 20 minutes until it reaches 235° (soft ball stage).

Remove from heat and stir 2 to 2½ minutes, beating well by hand, until it loses its gloss. Drop by spoonful onto wax paper or greased cookie sheet.

Finished candies should be smooth and flat. Store in airtight containers.

Note: Timing is all important in this recipe. Watch candy thermometer carefully.

Mrs. Archibald A. Farrar
(Emily Nixon)

Fruitcake Cookies

A nice change from traditional fruitcake at holiday
gatherings. Excellent served with ambrosia.

Preparation: Average   **Yield:** 11 Dozen
Cooking Time: 15 Minutes

8 cups pecans
1 pound candied pineapple
1 pound candied cherries
1 pound dates
3 cups self-rising flour
3 eggs
1 cup sugar
1 cup shortening
1 teaspoon rum flavoring
1 teaspoon lemon flavoring
1 teaspoon butter flavoring

Preheat oven to 325°.

Cut pecans and fruit into small pieces. This may be done in the food processor, but make sure to use flour with fruit for cutting.

Sift flour over fruit and nuts, mix well. Melt shortening. Beat together eggs, sugar, shortening and flavorings. Pour this mixture over fruit, pecans and flour and mix thoroughly with hands.

Grease cookie sheets. Drop dough with a tablespoon onto cookie sheet and press lightly.

Bake 15 minutes or until lightly browned. Be careful not to overcook.

Cool and store in airtight containers. These freeze well.

Mrs. Ray Dempsey
(Emmilyn New)

Chocolate Cups

This really gives a special effect with little effort.

Preparation: Average
Cooking Time: 5 Minutes

Yield: 6 Cups

3 squares semi-sweet chocolate
1½ teaspoons shortening
6 paper cupcake liners

Melt chocolate and shortening over hot water. Stir until smooth.

Remove from hot water and allow chocolate to cool until thick enough to spread. Watch closely.

Place fluted or plain paper cupcake liners in muffin tin. Spread chocolate onto bottom and around inside of liners with small rubber spatula.

Chill or freeze until firm. Carefully remove liners from chocolate cups.

Hint: For gift giving, package carefully and suggest filling with ice cream, mousse or fresh fruit.

Mrs. William M. Huffman
(Jo Gross)

Microwave Pecan Brittle

Preparation: Easy   **Yield:** 1 Pound
Cooking Time: 15 to 20 Minutes

> **1 to 1½ cups pecan halves**
> **¼ cup butter**
> **Salt to taste**
> **1 cup sugar**
> **½ cup corn syrup**
> **1 teaspoon butter**
> **1 teaspoon vanilla extract**
> **1 teaspoon baking soda**

Melt ¼ cup butter in an iron skillet.

Toss pecans in butter with a wooden spoon over low heat until crisp, about 5 minutes. Salt to taste after you remove from heat.

Mix sugar and corn syrup in an 8 x 12 inch glass baking dish. Microwave on high 4 minutes and stir with a wooden spoon.

Microwave 4 more minutes. Stir in pecans, butter and vanilla. Microwave 2 minutes on high.

Add soda and stir until light and foamy. Pour onto greased baking sheet and, working quickly, spread thin. Allow to cool and break into small pieces.

Store in airtight container in a cool place.

Mrs. James H. Vick, Jr.
(Charlotte Cummings)

138

Apricot Bars

Better made a day or two ahead!

Preparation: Average
Cooking Time: 55 Minutes

> **1 cup all-purpose flour**
> **¼ cup white sugar**
> **½ cup butter**
> **⅓ cup all-purpose flour**
> **¼ teaspoon salt**
> **½ teaspoon baking powder**
> **2 eggs**
> **1 cup brown sugar**
> **½ teaspoon vanilla extract**
> **½ cup chopped nuts**
> **⅔ cup dried apricots**
> **Confectioners' sugar**

Preheat oven to 350°.

Combine 1 cup flour, sugar and butter until crumbly. Pat into greased 9 x 9 x 2 inch pan and bake 25 minutes or until lightly brown.

Cut apricots into pieces with scissors and cook in small amount of water until apricots are soft.

Sift together ⅓ cup flour, salt and baking powder. Beat eggs and slowly mix in brown sugar. Add flour mixture and mix well. Add vanilla, nuts and apricots.

Spread this over baked layer. Bake 30 minutes or until done. Cool in pan and cut into bars. Roll in confectioners' sugar. Roll again in sugar after 30 minutes.

Mrs. John Liverett
(Nancy Lawton)

Graham Cracker House

Such a fun thing to do with children during Christmas holidays.

Preparation: Easy   **Yield:** 3 Houses
(Do not attempt on a rainy day.)
Cooking Time: None

1 (14 ounce) box graham crackers

Candies for decoration:
M & M's
Red Hots
Small gum drops
Mini-marshmallows
Life savers
Peppermint candy (small pillar type)

Fluffy Icing:
3 egg whites at room temperature
½ teaspoon cream of tartar
1 (1 pound) box confectioners' sugar

**1 piece of cardboard approximately
8 x 10 inches for base**

Construction:
6 graham crackers (2 right from box for the roof; 2 with 1 section (of a 4 section cracker) removed for the front and back of the house; 2 with one section removed and then top section cut to a peak for sides of the house to support roof. (Use sharp knife to cut.)

Icing:
Beat egg whites and cream of tartar until very foamy. Gradually add sugar and beat until stiff peaks form and icing holds a sharp line when knife is pulled through it. If it needs thinning, add a drop or two of lemon juice. Keep bowl covered with damp cloth to prevent any drying. Any presence of oil will break down icing.

To Assemble:
Apply icing to bottom edges of front, back and side crackers. Place on cardboard to form basic house construction.

Using icing decorator tube with small star tip, apply icing along center of roof and along edges of roof where it will meet the house. Reinforce seams with extra icing.

Draw on windows and door with decorator tube.

Now be creative and decorate your house with candy, using the icing as glue.

The leftover icing may be spread on the cardboard around the house and sprinkled with shredded coconut to resemble snow. Two marshmallows will make a snowman. Leftover crackers makes fences and benches.

Mrs. Will Cunningham
(Jane Owen)

140

Menus

Brunch

Orange Romaine Salad

Breakfast Sausage Ring

Sunday Morning Sweet Rolls

Sangria

Dinner Party

Mushroom Pastries

Chilled Cherry Soup

Salad with Brie Dressing

Rolled Leg of Lamb with Herbs

Baked Squash

Cloverleaf Ice Box Rolls

Biscuit Tortoni

Informal Luncheon

Cheese Straws

Special Chicken Salad

Fresh Fruit in Season

Black Forest Crêpes

Cook Out

Mixed Greens with Company Bacon Dressing

Ribs with Fourth of July Barbecue Sauce

Georgia Brunswick Stew

Sour Cream Rolls

Lemon Ice Cream with Raspberries

Country Store Soft Ginger Cookies

Index

146